# INFANTICIDE:

## ITS

## LAW, PREVALENCE, PREVENTION, AND HISTORY.

BY

# WILLIAM BURKE RYAN, M.D.(Lond.)

### F.R.C.S., Eng.,

FOTHERGILLIAN GOLD MEDALLIST FOR AN ESSAY "ON INFANTICIDE
IN ITS MEDICO-LEGAL RELATIONS" (1856).

"The subject is of great importance; and Lord Brougham recommends Dr. Ryan to send a full statement of the facts and of his
suggestions to the Meeting of the National Association for the
Promotion of Social Science."

## LONDON:

J. CHURCHILL, NEW BURLINGTON STREET.

——

1862.

LONDON: T. RICHARDS, 37, GREAT QUEEN STREET.

# PREFACE.

THE interest I have taken in the deplorable subject of infanticide is the result of no sudden impulse. In the year 1856 I was awarded the Fothergillian Gold Medal of the Medical Society of London for an essay *On Infanticide in its Medico-legal Relations.* The history of infanticide now glanced at is abridged from that manuscript.

In 1858, I published in the *Sanitary Review and Journal of Public Health*, an article, "Child-murder in its Sanitary and Social Bearings," and in forwarding a copy of this, amongst others, to Lord Brougham, as President of the Law Amendment Society, I was recommended by that illustrious nobleman—whose ardour neither age can subdue, nor a multiplicity of avocations prevent from giving a calm and anxious consideration to the numerous matters of the day,—to bring the subject before the meeting of the *National Asso-*

*ciation for the Promotion of Social Science*, to be held in Liverpool in October; saying, at the same time, that he had apprised the Secretary, Mr. Hastings, of his recommendation. An extract from his Lordship's letter is placed on the title page.

A desire from such a source I could consider little less than a command. I therefore went to Liverpool and read the paper at St. George's Hall, Lord Brougham himself presiding in consequence of the Lord Chancellor of Ireland, Mr. Napier, not being able to leave Ireland in time. Month after month passed, and various occupations prevented publication, although hourly intended. But now that the sad catalogue of infanticides daily increases, it would be improper to delay longer calling attention to the matter, with a hope that the people of England may at last make a successful effort to stem this horrid tide, and to relieve the country from a disgrace which at present lies heavily upon it; and the minds of individuals from a consciousness that a crime of a frightful nature —a crime that ought to be stayed—is very prevalent.

W. B. R.

16, *Norfolk Terrace, Bayswater,*

*June,* 1862.

# CONTENTS.

## PART I.

## PART II.

## PART III.

# INFANTICIDE.

WHEN we consider the gravity of the matters involved in Infanticide; the disgrace that may be brought on a community amongst which the crime is prevalent; the great interest that is at stake to the individuals concerned; but above all, the great law of nature which is so grossly outraged whenever systematic child-murder is committed; we must conclude that the subject is of the most vital importance to philanthropists of all creeds and nations, but much more to him on whose mind is thoroughly impressed, with unquestioning acquiescence in its propriety, the wisdom of the command, "*Thou shalt not kill.*" Our laws on the subject are in a most unsatisfactory condition.

The laws regarding infanticide have varied very much in this, as in other countries, at different periods. They were formerly of extreme severity all over the continent of Europe, and this very severity often rendered them nugatory, wholly counteracting their provisions. In France, for instance, in 1556, by an edict of Henry II, every unmarried woman who concealed her pregnancy, the death of her infant ensuing, was herself condemned to death. This law was peculiarly severe, as the death might have occurred from causes altogether unintentional. Immaturity of the infant was here a sufficient plea on the part of the accused. This law, like our own Act, 21 James I, which appears to have been modelled after it, has been modified. The Act of James, where a bastard child was found dead, required proof on the mother's part that the child was born dead. The woman was otherwise visited with punishment, and that punishment was death. The very severity of this law secured its overthrow.

By an Act of 1803, women tried for the murder of bastard children are to be tried by the same rules of evidence and presumption as are by law allowed to take place in other trials for murder; and here provision is made in case the first trial fails from want of sufficient evidence, to fall back upon a second trial for concealment of pregnancy; and unfortunately the very state of the law, backed by the commiseration often felt by the jury, seconded as it is by public opinion, renders this resource but too frequent. The punishment being death on conviction on the capital offence, and many circumstances making the jury disinclined, in individual instances, to this extreme, the trial for concealment is adopted, the punishment for which is two years imprisonment; and this is as little commensurate to the enormity of the offence, in many instances, as the other would be beyond it. The Act 9 Geo. IV modified this statute, and provided that it should not be necessary to show whether the child died before or after birth in cases where concealment of birth was proved.

In medical jurisprudence, infanticide means the murder of a new-born child, and there is no specific time named to which the term "*new-born*" applies, as it is not restricted to days after birth. Trials for infanticide take place as do those of ordinary murder, but there are some particular proofs required which make such trials differ from those of ordinary ones; and there is one proof especially demanded which, to the common-sense view of people, would appear as if brought in for the purpose of evading justice, which it very often does. For instance, proof is required that the child was "*wholly born*," and had an existence independent of its mother when it was killed. We shall see by and by what melancholy consequences

must result from such a demand, and how the
habits of a people and the morals of a nation may
at last come to be influenced by such a state of
law, as to make the sacrifice of infant life, if
not excusable, at least to be looked upon with less
feelings of horror than those with which murder of
any description should be contemplated. And indeed it is unhappily true that, from whatever cause
it may have arisen, infanticide is not looked upon
in the same light as other murders by the public
generally; and whether this feeling may have
caused or only seconded the state of the law, it is
equally to be lamented. The stream of prejudice
has altogether changed; and while formerly the
law was severe even to the extreme of injustice,
now it is so loose as to be little more than a
*mockery* of justice. There is no crime that meets
with so much sympathy, often of the most ill-
judged kind; and an almost partisan feeling has
frequently been evinced, not only by the legal, but
even by the medical profession.

In most cases of infanticide there are many obstacles thrown in the way of the medical witness,
and various doubts may arise of which the accused
may rightly claim the benefit. These obstacles
spring from the great difficulties of proving, in the
first instance, whether the child was destroyed;

these proofs depending on so many circumstances, varied in their nature, and on the results drawn from which, evidence of the most conflicting kind on the part of medical witnesses may be deduced. The difficulties to be encountered in proving, from the state of the lungs, whether the child has breathed or not, or to what extent respiration may have been carried; those to be met with in the evidence afforded by the state of the heart and lungs as to whether circulation of the blood may have commenced; those arising from the kind and position of wounds, and the question whether they were inflicted before or after death; those deriving origin from the maturity or immaturity of the infant, and the many other circumstances which, though beset with uncertainties and severe in themselves, are yet legitimate subjects of inquiry, to the full elucidation of which the prisoner has every claim; all these are sufficiently onerous on the part of medical witnesses, but quite justified by the peculiarities of the case, and the position of the accused: but when we come to the next proof required, as to whether the child was *wholly born* when the violence was committed, we feel that it is almost insurmountable; indeed, in most cases quite so. Let us see for a moment how much is included in this demand; and in doing so, I think we shall have reason to feel surprised that such a demand should ever have been made by "legislative wisdom," and that such a state of law should be laid down gravely from year to year; as well as that the good sense of the community has not rebelled against it, as seeing in it so plainly a "legal fiction"—a backdoor for the escape of a guilty and blood-stained mother.

It is not, then, sufficient that a medical witness prove that a child breathed at or about the time when violence was offered to it, *that it was alive in fact, and was killed.* This proof, one should think, would be all conclusive; but not so; for here, indeed, the chief difficulties commence. It is absolutely necessary, under the present state of the law, to prove that the child was *wholly born* when the violence had been committed,—that it existed independently of its mother. Hence it follows that the killing of a child during birth is not *murder in law;* that, in fact, a woman may kill her child, and provided only that any part of the child is within her own natural passages at the time, she cannot be brought in guilty of murder. A hand, a foot, an arm, still within the passages of the woman, screens the murderess from the penalties of murder. *Murder has been committed* in this state, and the murderess has been allowed to go at large, with an improved stock of experience for future need. On the heads of children being born into the world, their skulls have been broken in, or strangulation has put a period to their existence, and yet, because these children were not *wholly born*, the perpetrators have escaped; as if any difference existed in the moral turpitude of murdering a *partially* over that of a *wholly born* child!

A person can scarcely realize the fact that such is the state of the law in a civilized country; yet that it is so, has been frequently ruled. Baron Gurney stopped a case, when he elicited from the medical witness that a child might breathe during birth; and at the Norfolk Spring Assizes, 1837, Mr. Justice Coleridge ruled that the body of the child must be born in order to have an indictment for child-murder stand. Mr. Baron Parke has gone even farther. He said, at the Herts Lent Assizes, 1841, "With respect to all these cases, there is a degree of doubt whether the infant has been *born alive*. The law requires that this should be clearly proved, and that the whole body of the child should have come from the body of the parent. If it should appear that death was caused *during delivery*, then you will not find a true bill." Furthermore, a distinction has been made between *medical* and *legal* life; for, in 1845, an extraordinary case was reported, where Mr. Justice Erle laid down the law in this respect. In this case, proof was given that the child had breathed; and, in fact, when found, its head was nearly cut off. The jury were told that, before they returned a verdict of "guilty," they must be satisfied that the child had an existence distinct from, and independent of, the mother; that it was, in fact, *wholly born* when murdered by her: that the child might have respired before it came fully into the world, and that although such might be, *medically*, a live child, yet that it was not so *legally!*

What could the judge do? Such was the law. What could the jury do? Such were the judicial directions. But may we not ask, do not such a state of law, and the directions based upon them, outrage every feeling that we entertain of *a law*, human or divine? Is not such a state of things a disgrace to the statute-book? and is it not cruelty in the extreme to force a judge upon the bench into an enunciation of the law which he feels to be the merest mockery of justice? No one who has come to the use of reason can deny that, morally speaking, the person who kills a half, or partially born child, has blood-guiltiness stamped upon her fully as much as she who kills the wholly born one; and yet see what must be called the daring defiance of Divine admonitions in pronouncing the one party guiltless of offence, while the other is rightly considered punishable. The more such a state of things is pondered on, the greater is the surprise that it should be allowed to exist.

In the annals of criminal jurisprudence, some incredible dicta have arisen. It is but lately that a woman has escaped because the proof above named could not be given, although it appeared that, when the poor child was found, *pieces of its windpipe had been cut out.* In another case, in the year 1855, at Gloucester, a woman named Perry was charged with the wilful murder of her child. On the surgeon entering her room, she was in bed, with her head resting on the bolster, underneath which was a dead child, having its throat divided by some instrument. Here the surgeon could not positively say whether the child had been born alive, and under the direction of Mr. Baron Martin, the jury found they could not convict her of murder, and so fell back upon the only alternative the law allowed them in such cases,— trial for concealment of birth. A judge has even told a jury, that if they were of opinion that the prisoner had *strangled her child* before it was *wholly born,* they were bound to acquit her, and such indeed was the fact; but was not the circumstance in itself enough to bring the laws into disrepute, at the same time that such a state of things was calculated to incite to crime women desirous of getting rid of their children? And, let it be noticed, many women, who may feel inclined to rid themselves of a child, well know the state of the law,—well know that all the solemn preparations around them are but illusions; "empty sound, meaning nothing." For it is not always the young and previously artless girl, although covered with shame, that will be found to carry out an intention of murdering in its most cold-blooded form. Let such but have a mother's affections once stirred up within her, by the child being allowed to suckle her, and the infant is safe. It is rather with those who have been hardened in vice, and who may have had previous children, that the crime will be carried out more remorselessly; and with this class of people there is a talismanic sort of communication which alike informs them of the direction in which they are to seek abortion, or being unsuccessful in that, of the loopholes which the law has left, in its wisdom or its folly, in cases of infanticide.

Now it must be evident, at first sight, how almost

impossible it is in the generality of cases to prove that the child was wholly born, that no part whatever remained in the maternal passages when the violence which caused death occurred. In truth it is almost, if not quite, as much in the power of a non-medical as of a medical person to do that; and in order to a conviction in such cases, it would really be necessary that a person should be present to witness the deed, and depose as to the position of the child at the moment of injury. Surely, then, it is unfair towards a medical witness to require of him proof of what would be a nonsensical, if it were not a really criminal, legal quibble. A medical man is seldom or never in a position to give this proof. He has only to collect facts and circumstances; to sift, to weigh, and to depose to them. If there should be a doubt upon any one point, he should see that the prisoner gets the benefit of it, at the same time, he must not attempt to distort facts or circumstances for this purpose. In giving proof that the child was alive at the time that violence was offered to it, he discharges his part of the duty, and there his efforts should cease. If an inference, as to whether the child were *wholly born* or not, is to be made, the jury should make it,—they hold the scales, and should determine; but let the medical witness show no leaning one way or the other,—he has to depose to certain facts, and to answer certain questions.

More need not be said to show how ill-adapted is the present state of the law to deal with a certain aspect of infanticide, and to call public attention to it in order to its alteration. Better at once boldly proclaim immunity in cases of infanticide,—openly announce the morality of such deeds,—than to hedge them round with quibbles, which are only so many ingenious devices to secure the escape of the guilty. Of these devices, all the fictions concerning "live birth," "entire birth," or the "independent circulation of the child," partake; and openly to proclaim them as fictions would, at least, have the merit of a bold candour; while their retention, as part of the statute-law of the kingdom, is only a libel on truth and an insult to justice.

Let us for a moment take the case of an upright and conscientious judge, and we shall at once perceive how irksome it must be for such a man to be obliged to expound such a law as this, and to follow it literally, while all his better feelings revolt from the task.

It is not too much, then, to ask that the proof, whether a child were *wholly born* or not, when the violence which caused its death took place, be no longer required; but that proof that a child was alive at the time that the violence which caused its death was offered to it, be deemed sufficient to conviction in all cases of infanticide. Anything short of this is but a mockery,—a tampering with life, and an inducement to murder; and to this must we come unless, as is said by a most competent judge in matters of jurisprudence (Dr. Taylor), "we are prepared to admit that the destruction of a living and breathing child, *during* the act of birth, is not a crime."

See also how it affects a conscientious body of jurymen, every one of whom, perhaps, believes a prisoner guilty of murder; but because they have not proof of what the law stringently requires, that the child was *wholly born* when it was *murdered*, they acquit her!

Infanticide in Prussia, its detection and punishment, bear many resemblances to our own laws on the subject. In late years there have been several cases of infanticide in the district of Stralsund. In eight cases pregnancy was denied, parturition was concealed and the child destroyed. In one case the mother died; in two cases legal proceedings were stayed; in three the murderesses were declared not guilty by the jury; in one case a verdict equivalent to "not guilty" was returned, and in one case only was the culprit found guilty.

Paradoxical as it may appear, it is nevertheless true, that infanticide is permitted by the Prussian laws. By a clever use of the law as there administered, each unmarried pregnant woman may kill her child and remove it without becoming liable to punishment. She can deny her pregnancy, and knowing this she resists all inquiry and examination, to make which no one has a right. She must then quietly wait till her confinement. After birth the mother has only to cover her child with the bed-clothes, and thus induce death by asphyxia. The first breath can with difficulty be prevented. The hydrostatic test affords evidence if the child has breathed and lived. By good fortune the medical evidence may prove only that the child has *probably* lived and may have died of apoplexy, induced by pressure on the head during birth. There are no marks of injury. The fact of murder cannot be proved and proceedings are stayed. Or the case may come before a jury (Geschwornen), and as soon as they hear of anything "*probable*," or "*very likely*," or perceive the least hesitation on the part of the medical witnesses, they assuredly return a verdict of "Not guilty."

Dr. Haselberg, who gives the above account, further observes that, in a general way, jurors in that part of the world are not particularly acute as to the value of evidence, or the skill of medical witnesses. It is usual to summon a second or a third skilled witness, but this may only have the effect of rendering the evidence more doubtful. If there be a difference of opinion, the witness who is most popular or eloquent has most weight, though his opinion be of the least real value.

The state of the law as regards punishment is equally unfair towards the jury, and may account in some degree for their great unwillingness to convict on the capital offence. They must either convict the accused of murder, or acquit her. Even when the evidence is very strong, and the offence of a very aggravated character, the severe penalty attached to conviction sways the minds of juries; and it is a rare thing indeed that a conviction takes place on the capital charge, but the jury fall back upon the power left them, and return a verdict for concealment of birth. Many circumstances may in these melancholy cases appeal to the commiseration of the jury. The girl may be young, of an interesting appearance, and in a friendless position, and may have fallen by the arts of seduction and been abandoned in her necessities; or she may have had many friends and relatives of fair social position, the thoughts of bringing shame on whom may, in the jury's opinion, have racked the brain to madness : but whatever the cause, such is the fact, that juries are most unwilling to convict, and the consequence is that justice is too often robbed of its due ; encouragement to an immoral and sinful habit is unwittingly given, and a nation is disgraced by having a crime of an atrocious character become habitual.

Seeing, therefore, that the punishment being so heavy, this unwillingness to convict is a thing established ; and seeing, that in some cases an amount of cold-blooded design, carried out to the death, is but too visible ; amount of design, for which the punishment for concealment of birth, two years imprisonment, offers no commensurate infliction ; the law should be altered so as to enable a judge to mete out punishment according to the nature and degree of the crime.  To be able to find for the capital offence, " with extenuating circumstances," as in France, would meet this, and give the judge that discretionary power which is so desirable. The amount of offence proved could thus fairly be dealt with.  It must, however, be remarked, as a bad sign of the times, that we often find a culprit of whose determined guilt the most undoubted evidence has been given, escape not only the punishment of death, but even the poor punishment attached to concealment of birth ; and, having richly deserved the gallows, is handed over perhaps to a six months' imprisonment. How juries can reconcile such as this to their conscience is not for me to say; but it appears very inconsistent, and very unlikely to stamp with a proper reprobation a crime of great magnitude.

Our statistics on the subject of infanticide are in a very unsatisfactory condition in this country, and will continue to be so until it be required of coroners' courts to give in all cases proper returns; specifying the nature of the accusation, and the kind and amount of proof, together with the result. It is much to be deplored that such returns have not been demanded long before this. From these courts alone can proper materials be obtained wherewith to build up statistics. Such returns were moved for in the House of Commons in 1852, but were unfortunately never made. See Appendix, as given further on.

Lord Raynham moved, in the House of Commons, in 1857, for a return of the number of persons convicted of infanticide from 1852 to 1856 inclusive, together with the sentence passed upon each; if modified or reversed; and specifying, also, whether the verdict had been accompanied by a recommendation to mercy, and if so, the reason or reasons, if any, alleged, etc. Returns, not yet

C

printed, have been made, but they give very little information. The strange fact, however, appears in some of them, that the clerks of assize had no means of answering whether the sentences had been modified or reversed; as well as that it was not customary to minute the jury's recommendation to mercy! It may be remarked that these returns were for the absolute *convictions* for infanticide, not for the absolute trials, much less the trials for concealment of birth. There were sixteen convictions for murder, and but one capital punishment, and this on a person who killed his two children, aged five and seven years respectively. These murders cannot be called infanticides. The only case of a conviction for the murder of a child at the Surrey Lent Assizes, 1852, does not specify the punishment. Neither is it specified in another case at the same place, where a woman was convicted of manslaughter on an indictment charging her with infanticide.

We cannot ignore the fact that the crime of infanticide, as well as that of criminal abortion, is wide spread and on the increase. The perusal of the daily and weekly papers painfully convinces us of the fact, as well as that it will require a strong hand to put it down.

The *Legal Examiner*, 1853, says, " The ' Circuit

Calendars' exhibit, as usual, a number of cases in which infants have met their deaths at the hands of their mothers. There is a horrible resemblance between the nature of the circumstances attending these deaths; but there is one difference, that they are more numerous than they used to be. The public, as well as the judge and the bar, notice it; and Mr. Justice Coleridge pointed it out to the grand jury at Worcester. We shall soon rival the Chinese people in callousness to infant life."

The *Morning Chronicle* says, " The natural instinctive horror of blood, the reverential sense of the sacredness of human life, seems to be becoming extinct amongst the humbler classes."

Mr. Hilles, writing in the *Legal Examiner*, considers that the crime of infanticide has spread to a fearful extent, and seems to be extending rapidly amongst the humbler classes of society. He doubts whether the closing of foundling hospitals in this country has not been more injurious than otherwise to public morals.

In many papers the most exaggerated statements prevail as to the number of exposures and infanticides in London alone. The number has even been placed as high as eleven hundred yearly. That it is very great is but too certain. Mr. Coroner Wakley is reported to have said that three hundred deaths by infanticide take place annually in London, although many are returned as dying from other causes, such as "stillborn," "over-laid," etc. He says that with ten thousand pounds at his command he could put a stop to the system. Most assuredly should twice or ten times the amount be placed at his disposal on his pointing out any feasible means of so doing.

We often notice very suspicious-looking returns of deaths, such as "from suffocation," etc. ; and though such may be cases of accidental death, yet their frequent repetition must make them be looked upon with great doubt. Shortly after the above expression of Mr. Wakley was published, six cases of death from suffocation were given in the returns of the Registrar-General for one week, and *five of these were infants.*

It is necessary to recall attention to the painful impression made upon the public mind by the publication of the *Sanitary Inquiry Report, Supplement,* " Interment in Towns," 1843, by Edwin Chadwick, Esq. In the Manchester and Salford district there was little mystery observed about the fact that children were enrolled in burial clubs in order that their deaths by neglect or more culpable means might bring profit to their unnatural parents ; and where a feeling so execrable exists, it behoves the public well to watch and extirpate it as soon as possible. Weeds of that noxious description thrive apace. In the above district the minister expressed himself as often shocked by a common phrase amongst the women of the lowest class, in alluding to children—" Aye, aye, that child will not live ; IT IS IN THE BURIAL CLUB." The actual cost of a funeral was from £1 to £1 10s., and the allowance from clubs from £3 to £5 ; there was thus left a profit to tempt the unnatural parents. We see how this temptation was increased, when it is added, that it was customary to include a child in four or five of these burial societies. It came out in evidence that one man had actually insured such payments *in nineteen different burial clubs in Manchester.*

In one case the cause of death assigned by a man was deemed unsatisfactory, and the clerk to the union, Mr. Gardiner, refused to register the death. He made inquiry and found that the death of the child was attributed to wilful starvation. *This child had been entered in at least ten burial clubs,* and the parents had six other children who only lived from nine to eighteen months respectively. They had received twenty pounds, from several burial clubs, for *one of these children ;* and they expected to receive as much or more for the child, the subject of the present inquiry, who was allowed to die without medical aid. The jury concluded that the evidence of the parents was made up for the occasion and was not entitled to credit; and the verdict was, " Died through want of nourishment, but whether occasioned by a deficiency of food, or by disease of the liver and spine, brought on by improper food and drink, does not appear." After this verdict the parents enforced payment from *ten burial clubs, obtaining* £34 3s.

Mr. Coppock, of the Stockport Union, had two similar cases brought under his notice, and in which he prosecuted the parents for murder. In one of these cases no less than three children had been poisoned with arsenic, and the father and mother were tried on the capital offence. The mother was acquitted; the father found guilty and transported for life. He should have been hanged. In the other case the judge summed up for a conviction, but the accused father was, to the astonishment of every one, acquitted. The body of the child was afterwards exhumed, *and arsenic found in its stomach.* In consequence of the suspicions entertained, two of the children of the first case were exhumed and arsenic was found in their stomachs. In all the cases payments were enforced from the burial clubs. The superintendent-registrar remarked of these dreadful cases, what reminds one of the Hindoo and Chinese customs, that the girls, as being less likely in after times to be of service to the parents, were those usually sacrificed. The impression on the minds of the medical men of Stockport was that infanticides were there committed for the sake of the burial money. At Liverpool a woman named Eccles was convicted of the murder of one child, and was under charge of poisoning another. Immediately after the murders she went to demand a stated allowance of burial money from the employers of the children. Cases of culpable neglect of children insured in burial clubs had also been observed at Preston; and the collector of one of the most respectable burial societies of Manchester had strong grounds for believing that it had become a practice to neglect children for sake of the money allowed. The practice of insuring in a number of clubs was increasing.

The town-clerk of Stockport prosecuted in two distinct charges. One was the case of a girl of sixteen years of age, and unlikely, from her weakly condition, to be of service to her parent. In this instance a verdict of natural death was returned by a coroner's jury; but, on the body being exhumed three months subsequently, arsenic was found. The jury acquitted the prisoner, contrary to the summing up of Mr. Justice Coleridge. A verdict so extraordinary, it was remarked, could only be accounted for by the general feeling against capital punishments, which enables so many criminals, capitally indicted, to escape punishment. This man received £8 from burial societies. The other case involved no less than three distinct cases of murder. Robert Sandys and George Sandys with their wives were the accused, their own children being the victims. They were all in burial societies.

In a work called *Sudden Death*, by Dr. Granville, compiled from the annual reports of the registrar-general, some very important statistics are given. He concludes that the vast mortality of infants must be looked upon with great suspicion, and says that, "Frightful as this early destruction of infant life must appear in the abstract, I grieve to add that, as we come nearer to the present times, not only does the general amount of life thus extinguished as it were on the threshold, increase, but the increase appears under circumstances capable of inspiring grave suspicions of its not being altogether natural. Thus I find that the early destruction of life is greater in certain manufacturing districts than in purely agricultural localities. "In alluding to the verdicts of "Found dead"; "Suffocation from accidentally having taken too much mother's milk"; "Accidentally overlaid"; etc., etc., he says; "Now, in all these cases, where the preceding verdicts were delivered, either the children were illegitimate, or the parents steeped in poverty." He thinks that the large mortality of children under one year throughout England and Wales, during the years 1847, 1848, and 1849, amounting to 267,086, calls for some serious investigation into its origin and causes. In some parts of England, he adds, the manufacturing towns to wit, such as Manchester, Ashton, Preston, Leeds, etc., this early mortality may rightly be called frightful.

During the present month of September, Mr. Wakley, in holding two inquests on unfortunate children that had been murdered in the public streets, the one having its throat cut, and the other having perished through wilful negligence at its birth, again alludes to the subject of infanticide, and to the deplorable mortality of children; observing, that similar cases to the above, shocking to relate, are now subjects of daily inquiry among the metropolitan coroners; that it was terrible to contemplate the annual sacrifice of infants that took place in London, and hoping that the serious attention of philanthropists, and of society generally, would be called to the matter.

I am decidedly of opinion that this unwillingness to convict on the part of juries, in cases of infanticide, is much to be reprobated, as well as lamented. It gives a silent sanction to the detestable practice, and indirectly encourages a system which brings indelible disgrace upon a nation. I cannot conceive how men can imagine they discharge their duty towards the Almighty, who, in the face of the plainest evidence of guilt, allow every culprit to escape. Disguise the feeling as we may, there is no Christian nation that must not occasionally think that here or hereafter a heavy account will be demanded of that community that tolerates the commission of so fearful an offence. How any commiseration could sway the feelings of a jury in the case of culprits under the iniquitous burial club system, is well calculated to excite surprise. Sympathy for a class of parents who could coolly plan and plot, day after day, the murder of their innocent offspring is false indeed, and only tends to encourage such monsters in their bad tendencies.

The case is different with an unfortunate girl, maddened, perhaps, by overwhelming shame and sense of wrong; and all excuse that can be made, short of excusing actual murder, should be made for such. Let the innocent by all means be protected, and punishments of an extreme severity only be inflicted where murder is most clearly proved. Better a thousand guilty should escape than that one innocent should suffer. But when things are fully brought home; when a cool and premeditated murder is proven, then severe punishment should quickly follow. Let no maudlin sentiment prevail where the greatest sin against Omnipotence, and the grossest outrage against society is committed, and much may be done to stop the fashion that now prevails of murdering innocent children. The sorry habit of allowing such crimes to be committed with impunity is well known. When deeds bespeaking great atrocity are brought to light, let some severe—aye, if necessary, terrible examples be made, and the practice, like shoplifting and other kindred vices, may be stopped; and what cannot be counteracted from a feeling of religious responsibility, may be prevented through fear of human punishments.

Above all, let women feel that they are not to be visited with so much indignation for simple pregnancy as for murder; the one is a sin of the passions and may be repented of most sincerely the next moment, and through the force of good moral resolution never committed again; but the other destroys a life that nothing can recall, and the memory of which destruction, unless the party be

dead to every feeling of remorse, must haunt them
uneasily to the last moment of existence.  It is
not too much to say that it is the bounden duty of
a nation to save persons inclined to this crime even
from themselves, and to protect the guiltily-in-
clined conscience from being seared by the commission of the deed.  Let society, if possible, look
on the fact of illegitimate pregnancy with a more
forgiving eye, and pity, at all events, the unhappy
victims of a systematic seduction, or the otherwise
innocent who may have fallen.  Let the future course
of life of such victims be of a less hopeless character : let them feel that an occasional flower may
be scattered on the thorny path that lies before
them, and that a green spot may now and then
glad their eyes and give rest to their limbs ; that
life is not to be of so wholly unendurable a character as they may suppose ;  that it may be no
longer from their own sex, that

> " Every woe a tear may claim,
>     Except an erring sister's shame."

and much may be done to lessen the evil.  The
moral criminality of such deeds should, by every
possible means, be kept steadily before the people.
This would be a meritorious work to undertake ;
and there are two parties in the state well calculated, from their social position, to undertake such

a work. I am speaking to a Christian people on a matter that deeply concerns themselves; and though one of the last to enlist religious tendencies in what, at first blush, might appear purely temporal matters, I feel that this is a business on which we must take higher than temporal views. I am, therefore, justified in asking the public, on the broad principles of Christianity, while we view the practice of infanticide as a flagrant crime against society, to look on it still more as an inexcusable sin against the Almighty. Let the minds of the people be thoroughly imbued with this truth, and legislation will be comparatively easy; let them be unaffected by its force, and the difficulty will ever remain:—legislation will be wanting in one of its greatest aids, and people will only require an opportunity to follow the bent of their evil tendencies.

One of the parties I allude to is the Medical Profession, whose power for working good, on this as well as on most other social questions, cannot be overrated,—a profession which has ever shown itself anxious to benefit suffering humanity, and disinterested in its endeavours. To them I appeal, merely mentioning the noble example left them by their heathen predecessor and professional father, *Hippocrates*, who took an oath, still called after his name, and demanded the same from his disciples, that he would never procure abortion.

The second party is the clergy, and their position and opportunities render their efforts, if rightly employed, all-powerful for good. They should never rest while so extensive a field is open before them; and while the prevalence of the crime is wide-spread and undoubted, they run the risk of neglecting their sacred mission the moment they cease to battle against it. No time should be considered inappropriate, no society should be considered too exalted, in which to proclaim the iniquity of the practice. Thus would the civil power be ably and successfully seconded, and thus would the torrent of infanticide be stemmed, In this respect former examples are sufficiently consoling, when it is considered that Christianity, both in its early ages, as well as in its latest efforts in India, has done more than all other institutions, and even in despite of almost all other institutions, to abolish the crime.

What, then, are the best means for preventing infanticides? First, moral teaching; then, general teaching; then wise laws, prompt to punish the guilty as beneficent in protecting the guiltless; forbearing to drive the poor sinning female into the desert as a scapegoat laden with the sins of a pharisaical community ; a sincere and charitable attempt to make women more independent and therefore more self-reliant—not unfeminine, for in that would they lose the chief charm of their sex. That dependence which they must ever have upon man as the stronger and more indomitable animal, ever ready to meet danger and prompt to avert it, is to be met, not by an emulation for which their weaker physical frame is unfitted, but by those fond and considerate kindnesses, and that trusting confidence which peculiarly belong to their sex ; and which make them in their very weakness often more influential and more powerful than the opposite sex in all its boasted manhood.

After much study of the matter, and comparing the opinions and statistics of many different authorities, I am inclined to think that foundling hospitals conduce much to the prevention of the crime of infanticide. I think that the great weight of opinion tends to this view. Whether they are adapted to the "genius" and habits of this country is a point which need not at present be discussed. The great objections that they may be abused, as when married parents, too lazy to support their children, wish to desert them ; or that they lead to immorality as to sexual intercourse ; or finally that the mortality is undeniably great—I consider

light in the scale—if they only put a stop to the
more monstrous vice,—the more crying evil. I
can well imagine, although I am far from admitting, that greater laxity of morals as to this intercourse may lead to more illegitimate births in
countries where they exist; but I cannot believe
that infanticides are likely to occur in equal numbers where hospitals are supported as in those
countries where they do not exist. Such a conclusion would argue too strongly for the depravity
of human nature, and a person may well be ex-
cused in not arriving at it. These institutions
were doubtless established to prevent exposures
and infanticides, and in common with all other institutions for the amelioration of human misery
were from time to time fearfully abused, and this
to such an extent as to demand their suppression;
but this was followed by such an increase of exposures and infanticides that recourse was again
obliged to be had to them. This was especially
the case in France in the reign of Louis XIII. In
speaking of them as giving rise to immorality, is
it not possible that we are taking the effect for the
cause, and that we are excluding climate, which
notoriously influences the passions, in making up
the account? Many of the abuses of such could
be remedied by a proper amount of supervision—

indeed, such have been remedied where a strict system of registration has been adopted. Touching infanticides, Dr. Webster, whose statistical inquiries are entitled to great weight, mentions the extraordinary circumstance, that when he recently visited Sweden, he found of 1183 persons, lately undergoing punishment in the prisons, 106 were committed for infanticide and twenty-six for procuring abortion, being one-ninth of the inmates of these establishments! I am not aware that such things have been shown to exist where foundling hospitals are established. He also mentions the large proportion of illegitimate children born in Stockholm; one-third of the whole births being bastards! By a recent return in his possession, out of 4614 births registered in Stockholm during one year, 1424 were illegitimate, nearly 31 per cent! This strongly shows the connexion between illegitimacy and infanticide. This account, however, differs much from that of the Registral-General given below as to Sweden generally.

The registration of illegitimate births cannot in all cases be taken as a criterion of the morality of a locality; for, in the Registrar-general's reports, London figures but as 3·2 per cent., while other parts of the country show a proportion of 18·1 per cent., as at Wigan; or 13·8, 12·2, 12·0 in

Nantwich, Nottingham, and Ormskirk respectively. Now in London, where the standard of morality is not over high, many things exist to account for this low per centrge. For instance, the class of women with whom illicit intercourse takes place is not likely to procreate as in the country. Illegitimacy must be calculated by counties, if not by countries generally, rather than by isolated localities. It would be useless to take the extremes above given, as it would be in the case of Vienna where bastardy is so extensive, and Austria generally, where it figures still very high.

Geraudo gives statistics of illegitimate births per 1000 in countries with, and in those without hospitals for foundlings.

### STATES WITHOUT HOSPITALS.
Illegitimate births per 1000.

| | |
|---|---|
| Prussia . . . . . | 69 |
| England and Wales . . . | 55 |
| Wales alone . . . . | 83 |
| Saxony . . . . . | 121 |
| Hesse . . . . . | 149 |

### STATES WITH HOSPITALS.
Illegitimate births per 1000.

| | |
|---|---|
| France . . . . . | 71 |
| Naples . . . . . | 46 |
| Archduchy of Austria . . | 42 |

Terme and Monfalcon, Remacle, Guerry, Benoiston de Châteauneuf, etc., give many statistics regarding illegitimacy in France, showing, that in the beginning of the present century, the illegitimates were to the legitimates as 1 in 20; at present as 1 in 14, and it is considered that the wars and conscriptions of the first part of the century would account for the disproportion. From 1824 to 1833, the legitimate births in France were 9,031,908; illegitimate, 703,663; while the foundlings were 336,281. In 1847, the legitimate births are placed at 918,581; the illegitimate at 65,626. The increase of population is considered fairly to account for the increase of foundlings.

We have more recent statistics in the reports of our own Registrar-general, as follows:—

### PROPORTION OF 100 CHILDREN BORN.

|  | Legitimate. | Illegitimate. |
|---|---|---|
| Sardinia | 97·909 | 2·091 |
| Sweden | 93·438 | 6·562 |
| Norway | 93·322 | 6·678 |
| England | 93·279 | 6·721 |
| Belgium | 93·228 | 6·772 |
| France | 92·885 | 7·114 |
| Prussia | 92·878 | 7·122 |
| Denmark | 90·649 | 9·351 |
| Hanover | 90·124 | 9·876 |
| Austria | 88·620 | 11·380 |
| Wurtemberg | 88·260 | 11·740 |
| Saxony | 85·003 | 14·997 |
| Bavaria | 79·402 | 20·598 |
| Lombardy | 96·1 | 3·9 |
| Venice | 97·5 | 2·5 |

That the mortality of foundling hospitals is very great is unfortunately too true; and such, even under the most favourable circumstances, will ever be the case where outcasts are reared with all the attendant disadvantages of a mother's absence. It can be shown that illegitimate children, in or out of such institutions, are far from having as many chances in their favour as legitimate ones, either as regards being reared, or subsequent advancement in the world. But any institution, no matter how great its mortality, that will only prevent the stain of murder settling upon a nation, is, in my opinion, to be hailed as a boon. If we take all things into consideration, the poverty of the mothers of most bastard children, the neglect to which with such mothers they should be exposed, and the thousand difficulties under the circumstances in the way of rearing them, we must leave a very large margin for mortality during the first year. The mortality before birth, says the *Registrar-general*, and in the first year after birth, is, in many countries, *sixty or seventy per cent. higher among illegitimate than among legitimate children.* Even amongst all, legitimate and illegitimate, in very poor and crowded localities, the mortality is very high, as in some parts of Paris it amounts to 32 per cent. In similar localities in London to 33·1 and 29 per cent., if we take Lambeth and Poplar (1848) respectively. More startling facts come to light in still later times, and it is computed that 5000 children under five years of age are lost annually in London, and these chiefly from preventable causes. Like, as in some foundling hospitals, much of this mortality is owing to children being brought up by hand; the want of mother's milk appears the great cause of the destruction of infants. In a report of the medical attendant to an east end parish, it is computed that 49 per cent. of the whole mortality of the district was composed of children. The evils in this respect are really appalling. In Leeds, the mortality of children under one year has been 30·6 per cent ; and in Preston, during the strike (1853-4), 33·3 per cent. In some parts of Russia the mortality is 31 per cent., and of an average of 27 throughout the empire.

Tables of the mortality of foundlings have been given—as at St. Petersburgh, 40 per cent. under one year ; Florence, 40 per cent. ; Barcelona, 60 ; Paris, 80 ; Marseilles, 90 ; Dublin, 91. In France generally, in 1824, they were 57·6 per cent. In these institutions many causes combine to this vast mortality. The secrecy which is so indispensable in all proceedings connected with illegitimate children render their removal—in darkness and in silence—be the weather good, bad, or indifferent, a cause of peculiar mortality. The carelessness of paid messengers who have no interest in the poor children; the diseases peculiar to all hospitals, as well as epidemic and other diseases, all add their adverse influence. But, as has been observed of those poor children in London, the absence of mother's milk plays the greatest part in the destruction of infant life. This is proved at Parthenay and Poitiers, where the children in the Foundling Hospitals are suckled, as is also the case at Lyons; and where the mortality is much less than at a place called X, where they are brought up by hand.

Prizes have been offered in France for the best essays on the sources of mortality and for suggestions of remedies; one, the Monthyon, was conferred on MM. Terme and Monfalcon for their treatise. Prizes offered for essays on the causes of mortality amongst our own infant population, with suggestions for its prevention, would be very desirable.

That deplorable and all-absorbing love of gain, which forms one of the most repulsive characteristics of the age, leans particularly heavy on some of the female portion of the community. The unfortunate state of things in what may be called

unskilled labour, which makes so many toil day
and night, till brain and heart and mind are alike
overpowered, confused and worn out, in working
for a miserable stipend which can scarcely be said
to support existence, is melancholy in the extreme.
To have any human being making shirts, waist-
coats and mantles from three-halfpence to three-
pence each is a saddening spectacle; yet in doing
this and such like are many of the most interesting
of their sex, whose gentle natures calmly buoy
them up while the wear and tear of existence literally consumes the physical frame which the food
to be bought by their scanty earnings gives them
no adequate means to replenish. It is an absolute
fact that at this sad and weary needlework the
eyes themselves are worn out, and amaurotic
blindness ensues; the insufficiently nourished and
impoverished heart, in order to make up for its
healthy action, doubles and trebles its efforts, and
at last runs down exhausted; the lungs themselves,
sickened as it were, and obstructed by the impure
atmosphere on which they are obliged to live, leave
the blood whose integrity carries health to the
system, impure and poisonous, and finally fatal to
life, and are themselves blocked up by refuse and
*debris* which destroy their very texture. Another
kind of unskilled labour, too, that of the poor go-

verness, brings but little remuneration for the toils
and privations, and even the still more painful slights
to which that class is subject. Her position, like
that of the other, peculiarly lays her open to the
chances of a systematized seduction, and its consequent hopelessness and ruin; a state of things
which too often leads to infanticide. Women have
not yet taken their proper position in the labour-
market, and many trades are open to them for
which they are peculiarly fitted, such as watch-
making, and many of the lighter trades. They
appear to be shoved even off the stools which
should be their own especial birthright by men of
brawny shoulders and strong limbs. The modesty
of lady customers would be quite in as safe keeping if served by their own sex in matters of delicacy. There are numberless things at which
women could earn money without interfering with
domestic expectations, which should not be disap-
pointed, for when a woman is married and has a
family, she owes as much to the comfort of her
husband, and proper care of her children, as will
probably occupy all her time; and this comfort
and this care will be none the less by her having
previously been able to earn her own livelihood.
The very fact that she has done so will give a zest
to her exertions and a system to her industry.

Education in the domestic relations and requirements themselves is also a desideratum of the greatest importance, for there are some women so ignorant of how they should add to their own or their husband's comforts by a wise economy or systematic management, that they are really more a clog upon progress than anything else. There is also another class of young women, or young "*ladies*," as they are called, belonging to the semi-genteel divisions of society, that are really most worthless for any kind of good. In this class may be seen the daughters, perhaps, of a man with from two to four hundred a year, depending on his exertions for that, and which ceases of course with his life, with a house full of these "young ladies," who "sew not, neither do they spin;" who spend the last shilling in their father's coffers in flimsy and tawdry dress, and spend their time at worthless acquirements, or in swallowing the distorted sentiment of trashy novels; but who, while ever on the look out, even to the forlorn hope, that "something will turn up" in the shape of a husband, are utterly unfit for any exigency of the married life. They have scarcely the knowledge or the energy to boil a potatoe.* The members of this

---

\* On one of the days of the great Social Science Meeting at Liverpool, Lord Shaftesbury said, that he at one time went through " the streets of a Lancashire town, and out of twenty-class, and it is a large one, as well in towns as amongst certain denizens of the country, while they are looked on with contempt by those above them, whose means and position render them independent, are a bad example to those below them, who are but too often tempted to ape their emptyness and imitate their vanity, until their morals and their virtue are at the mercy of the first comer.

There is another thing which presses hard upon the poor outcast mother of an illegitimate child, and which in itself forms one of the greatest inconsistencies. It is that the law can only enforce payment of *two and sixpence* a week\* from the

---

five houses in the street which he examined, he could not find one single woman who could mend a shirt, or darn a stocking, or cook the smallest dish for her husband and children."

\* And even this 2s. 6d. a week, owing to the imperfect working of the bastardy laws, is not always to be secured. There is often great difficulty in finding the fathers, and the relieving officers cannot interfere. The mother is thus forced upon the parish. According to the statement of Mr. Tubbs, there were some time ago, eighty-five persons receiving the weekly pittance of one shilling each from the parish of St. Mary-le-bone, because they could not or did not recover from the fathers.

It has been further stated that, on the 1st of January, 1858, no less than 14,427 children were charged, under similar circumstances, on the parochial rates in 629 unions and single parishes in England and Wales, out of the then existing population of 16,621,399 souls.

In England, in 1857, 5,816 men were taken into custody for disobeying bastardy orders in the year 1856. The old poorlaw gave power to the parish to recover from the fathers. This power ought to be resumed by the present law.

putative father for a certain number of years. Now this applies as well to the man who may have, without a single exertion, thousands a year, as to the poor working man who may on an average not be able to earn more than *thirty pounds* a year. Surely the father should be compelled to pay according to his means, so that the amount does not act as an inducement to immorality on the part of young women. At present £6 10s. is the allowance, and that might be still left as the minimum, as it is as much as some can pay; but there are circumstances of peculiar hardship in some cases, where, for instance, a young and innocent girl, who may not be under the protection of her father when misfortune overtook her, cannot have an action for seduction brought, because that father lost none of her services; and in such a case provision should be made for the child in some degree commensurate to the means of the father. For the amount at present allowed no woman can put her child out to nurse. She is, therefore, tied down neck and heels to attend to this child herself—all chance of future exertion is denied her—down, down she is chained to the muddiest bank of society, until the most ardent and virtuous hopes for future reformation are thrown aside in despair, and the once innocent and really modest—from whom the momentary cloud might have been removed with the effect of rendering the woman again desirable for society—is left to struggle as an outcast, with all the feelings engendered by such a fate. In all cases, however, good proof should be required, that an innocent man be not made the victim.

I would, in conclusion, ask,—1st. That in cases of Infanticide, proof that the child has been "*wholly born*" be no longer required, but that in all cases it be sufficient to prove that the child *met its death by violence.* 2nd. That, as in the French law, the jury may find upon the capital charge "with extenuating circumstances"; and that punishment *according to the nature of the circumstances attending the crime* be justly meted out. 3rd. That in order to enable the mother of an illegitimate child to free herself for future exertions, the putative father be obliged, according to his circumstances, to pay such a sum as will enable the woman to put the child out to nurse; and that this sum vary, from the present amount as a minimum, to seven and sixpence per week, according as circumstances of aggravation, which the law may not otherwise be able to meet on behalf of the woman, may appear.

# II.

## INFANTICIDE AND ABORTION FURTHER CONSIDERED.

HAS infanticide, then, diminished since the above paper was read? Have we reason to congratulate ourselves upon the fact that the slaying epidemic has passed from over the face of the land, or is on the decline? Alas, no ! on the contrary, the feeble wail of murdered childhood in its agony assails our ears at every turn, and is borne on every breeze. The sight is horrified as, day after day, the melancholy catalogue of murders meets the view, and we try to turn away the gaze in the hope of some momentary relief. But turn where we may, still are we met by the evidences of a wide spread crime. In the quiet of the bedroom we raise the boxlid, and the skeletons are there. In the calm evening walk we see in the distance the suspicious-looking bundle, and the mangled infant is within. By the canal side, or in the water, we find the dead child. In the solitude of the

wood we are horrified by the ghastly sight; and if
we betake ourselves to the rapid rail in order to
escape the pollution, we find at our journey's end
that the mouldering remains of a murdered innocent have been our travelling companion; and that
the odour from that unsuspected parcel too truly
indicates what may be found within.

The medical and daily press give painful evidence how widespread is the crime of Infanticide,
and of the feelings of uneasiness and alarm under
which the public mind labours. People stand
aghast at the facts they witness; men's minds are
bewildered; and scarcely dare the question be
asked, "Can nothing be done to stop this frightful
evil?" or if occasionally asked, scarcely is there
as yet a response; people are astounded, but dare
not make an effort to escape the painful load under
which they groan; and they sink into unworthy
apathy until the next glaring massacre horrifies
them into temporary action. And is this as it
should be? and is this the becoming attitude of a
matter-of-fact and business-like nation, to which
the transactions of millions are but the consideration of a moment,—whose richly-laden vessels float
on every sea, and whose martial prowess is known
in every land? of a nation that poured out blood
and treasure in order to destroy the murderous

trade in slaves,—that trade which still, above all others, stamps with indelible disgrace the nations which openly proclaim its necessity or secretly perpetuate its horrors—a disgrace that more especially covers the people of America, because there does its stronghold exist, and because there a land is held up, of all others, as "a land of liberty." But it is not so; and it is a libel on humanity to call any land a land of liberty where the accursed trade in human beings is an institution, and where yells of human agony respond to the whip and the scourge. Still less is it the becoming attitude of a nation that may only now be said to have ceased from its Herculean task—and ceased only because of its full success—of destroying that system in India which made infanticide an institution, and which counted its victims by hundreds of thousands.

The day cannot be far distant when means will be taken to grapple with the system of infanticide in this country; and surely there can be no lack of wise or good men to form a *Commission of Inquiry* to probe this foul ulcer to the bottom, and to seek and find a remedy. No nobler work of charity can be undertaken,—no surer sign of patriotism need be sought. Never may the nefarious doctrine of Malthus take root in this or any other

Christian country, that "an occasional child-murder, from false shame, is saved at a very high price, if it can only be done by the sacrifice of some of the best and most useful feelings of the human heart in a great part of the nation." The enunciator of such a maxim was simply a murderer in his heart, and should be pronounced infamous !

A noble example has been set us in France, where the difficulties of dealing with the question of Foundlings and Infanticide were also known to be very great. Prizes were offered by different societies in order to the investigation of the subject, and much information was obtained. In 1838, the *Monthyon* prize of the French Academy was bestowed, as before mentioned, on MM. Terme and Monfalcon for their statistical history. Several other essays were sent in, which treat of Foundlings with great minuteness, and to which subsequent allusion shall be made. Surely a prize, worthy of laborious investigation, should be at once offered, in this country, for the best essay on the Prevention of Infanticide.

From the Bench we hear the warning voice. In a trial for concealment of birth, 20th August, 1858, the judge, Mr. Prendergast, Q.C., says, "We might talk about India, but he was sorry to say infanticide was carried on to a great extent in this country, and strong measures should be taken to repress it. Incontinence was one thing, and child-murder another."

In January, 1860, Mr. Justice Keating says; "This class of offences is much on the increase. Here, in the case of Charlotte Hubble, Dr. King and his assistant swore positively that the child was *born alive*. The body of a remarkably fine full-grown child, *still warm*, was found in the pri-soner's box, and round its neck twisted four or five times, and firmly tied, was a piece of tape. The jury returned a verdict of '*Not guilty*' of the murder, and this though they *took an oath* to *find according to evidence*."

Over and over again has the *Lancet* called atten-tion to the growing and wide-spread evil of infanti-cide. Over and over again has it dwelt upon the melancholy circumstances which give this country at present so painful a pre-eminence as regards this crime, and repeatedly has it appealed to public justice to step forward and stop the custom. "It has been ascertained," it says, in September 1861, "that in London alone within the last five years the bodies of 500 children have been found under such circumstances as could leave no doubt that their lives had been intentionally sacrificed. Up-wards of sixty were taken from the Thames, or

E

from the neighbouring ponds and canals. More than 100 were discovered stowed away under railway arches, upon the door-steps of houses, or in cellars or other out of the way places. Without exception in such cases as these, the children, if not dead when placed there, must have been deserted with the hope that death would speedily ensue."

The *Medical Times and Gazette*, too, in many able articles has rivetted attention on the subject, and loudly appealed for protection for the unhappy innocents. The medical periodicals, and the medical press generally, have warmly taken up the subject, and there can be little doubt that, in any efforts made to check the tendency to this crime, medical journalism and medical men, ever foremost in acts of protection and safety for their kind, will throw all their strength into the cause.

The daily and weekly press, too, metropolitan and provincial, has, time after time, kept the subject vividly before the public. The *Daily Telegraph* has lately had some ably-written articles on infanticide, working up the subject in a manner that shows its whole soul in the cause of its suppression. Most nobly has it appealed to the public sympathy. Having given some statistics, it remarks, " but there is reason to fear that they only give an approximative idea of the illegitimate infant population, and more especially of the extent to which infanticide prevails. How many tiny corses, how many baby skeletons, may be rotting and mouldering away now in secret places? How many women are there apparently virtuous and respectable, but whose countenances shew a hidden sorrow—a suppressed grief—whose life is one long conflict with conscience — one dreadful struggle with remorse for the deed that they have done— the deed that has been successfully concealed from the justice of man, but which God has seen and God will avenge. How," it asks, "shall we as a Christian, as a civilised, as a benevolent people, put an end to this widely-spreading sin of infanticide? Is it not time for our philanthropists to think upon the necessity for establishing a new and *genuine* Foundling Hospital—a charity such as exists in St. Petersburg and Moscow? It has been argued that the indiscriminate reception of foundling children would encourage immorality. Which is better—a little immorality or a great deal of infanticide? Which is preferable—a slight laxity of manners or wholesale wilful murder?"

The *Times*, also, has frequently brought powerful articles to bear on the subject. Indeed, the press generally has shown itself so fully alive to the subject, that the most sanguine hopes may be entertained of its continued watchfulness and support.

The *Standard* proclaims the sense of shame and guilt that exists ; and, in allusion to foundling hospitals, says, "First, it is requisite that the cruel, wicked, and unnatural theory that foundling hospitals must not be encouraged because the indiscriminate reception of children might possibly lead to a laxity of manners, must be abolished. It would be better, in the sight of God and man, that a thousand children should be born illegitimate, than that *one* innocent babe should be murdered by its distraught and desperate mother. But the thousand illegitimates need not be born. Leaving the gates of a foundling hospital open for that proportion of castaways, which will be the result of unbridled passions so long as human nature remains unregenerate human nature, the number may be reduced to an enormous extent if society will only relax its savage and hypocritical rules ; if the middle classes will encourage their sons to marry whether they have five hundred a year or not, instead of conniving at their continuance in profligate celibacy ; if society will set its ban not on the seduced victim, but on the barbarous seducer ; if clergymen will talk a little less to women

who have once lapsed from chastity about the fire
unquenchable and the worm that never dies, and
talk a great deal more to men whose career has
been one long course of systematic debauchery,
and at whose genteel depravity society points with
no finger of opprobrium, of the hell they have
made upon earth, and the hell they are preparing
for themselves in the Great Hereafter."

Amongst metropolitan parishes Marylebone
seems particularly unfortunate in being a *focus* of
child-murder. "Scarcely a week goes over," says
the *Marylebone Mercury*, "without the return of
evidence proving that this most affecting infringe-
ment of the natural laws, and heinous offence
against the laws of the realm, is on the increase."

"The practice of infanticide in Marylebone,"
says the *Medical Times and Gazette*, August 18,
1861, "still flourishes to a frightful extent. The
guardians of the poor last week passed a resolution
offering a reward of twenty-five guineas for the
discovery of the parent, or the person who exposed
the child, etc.; this being, as was stated, the
fourth case of child-murder within a short period
in that parish."

The Marylebone papers have for months been
full of this subject, which has been repeatedly
brought before the board of guardians by its different members.

Dr. Thompson, in his monthly report, Nov. 1860, on the health and climate of Marylebone, says, "A newly-born infant was found dead in the ornamental water, Regent's Park, wilfully murdered! I have not yet learned that any further steps have been taken respecting these cases. Surely, if there were a public prosecutor, it would be his duty to endeavour to discover the perpetrators of murders; or, in the absence of such a functionary, is there no one to investigate judicially such cases of child-murder as form the opprobrium of our parish month by month? Ten instances of the murder and manslaughter of infants are recorded in my annual report for 1859, and I have not heard of a conviction having taken place in the case of any of the murderers. Surely, if these crimes are not detected, something should be done to investigate and modify their causes."

The *Daily Telegraph* of August 15, 1861, gives an account of two inquests held by Mr. Brent upon two children, to one of whom, tied in a bundle, attention was drawn by the barking of a dog, as its owner was crossing Goldsmith's Paddock, Regent's Park. The other was found within the enclosure of Cavendish Square, wrapped in a black silk apron.

From Paddington, too, we learn that on one

Saturday no less than three cases of child-murder were reported by the authorities to the coroner. The first child was found within the enclosure of Sutherland Gardens; the second wrapped up as a bundle in Upper Hyde Park Gardens; and the third, with evidence of having been drowned, concealed in a bed-room of No. 15, Craven Hill Gardens. And we also find the following:—

"*A Murdered Child.*—On Tuesday, Mr. Brent held an inquest at the Dudley Arms, Harrow Road, Paddington, on the body of a female child. A rush basket was found in a third-class carriage, on the 11th of January last. It was removed into the cloak-room of the Paddington Station from the West Midland train, when, on Friday, an offensive odour was discovered, which was found to proceed from the basket. The basket was then opened by a porter, when a dead child was found to be the contents. It was of full period, and had lived seven or eight days. The body had been put into the basket warm, and there was a bruise on the right cheek-bone, and a graze lower down, but no fracture of the skull. The child had received no nourishment for thirty or forty hours before its death. The cause of death was the blow on the head, and insufficient nourishment. Verdict, 'Wilful murder against some persons or person unknown.'"

Even while writing (March 6, 1862), the following startling announcement is taken from a morning paper.

"*Suspected Infanticides.*—Mr. Brent, the deputy-coroner for West Middlesex, received information yesterday for inquests on the bodies of three newly-born infants, supposed to have been murdered. The first body was found in Hyde Park, carefully done up in a brown paper parcel, and taken to the dead house of St. George's, Hanover Square; the second was that of a fine child found wrapped in flannel and paper on a doorstep of a house in Sussex Place, Paddington; and the third was discovered wrapped up in the form of a parcel, lying in a garden at Maida Hill West. All these bodies were deposited in the Paddington deadhouse."

The daily press of the 2nd April announces the discovery, beside the Regent's Canal, of a bundle containing a *decapitated child!* The *Daily Telegraph* of April 11 reports no fewer than *five cases* of alleged murder, which were reported to the coroner the day before; and that of the twelfth announces two more. The *Hammersmith Reporter* of the latter date gives an account of another child found at Turnham Green, wrapped up in a bundle, with evident signs of strangulation.

"The parishes of Marylebone and Paddington," says the *British Medical Journal*, March 1861, "are especially infamous as seats of such massacres of the innocents." It adds that the deputy coroner suggested foundling hospitals as the most effectual means of checking the evil. This the *Journal* calls a "clumsy piece of mediæval machinery!" So much for a short-sighted prejudice. Mediæval machinery was powerful in preventing infanticide; modern machinery, if invented, remains rusting on its hinges—lifeless in itself, it seems hopeless to appeal to it.

In the papers of January 1, 1862, we find, "*The Strange Discovery of the Bodies of Two Children.*—Yesterday an inquest was held by Mr. Brent, at Chelsea Workhouse, on the bodies of two newly-born infants, found in a trunk, in a room at No. 2, Oakley Square, occupied by Agnes Renton, now in custody on a charge of concealment of birth. Mr. Thomas Dickson, medical officer of the workhouse, deposed that the bodies presented the appearance of being very old, and closely resembled mummies. Both were newly-born, the largest apparently a boy. He thought they were born alive, and at the full period, but their births must have dated years back. A cord was tied tightly in knots round the throat of each. He would not swear they were born alive. The deputy coroner said that at once defied their verdict, and there was nothing to be done in the case beyond returning an open verdict, and leaving it to the police to make a charge of concealment of birth. The jury acquiesced in the deputy coroner's opinion, and returned an open verdict, in effect that on the 26th of December each of the said children was found with cord tied tightly round his neck, in a certain box, at 2, Oakley Square, but whether born alive or not there was insufficient evidence to prove."

In Westminster we have the "*Supposed Murder of Two Children*—Yesterday, Mr. Bedford, coroner for Westminster, held an inquiry at Westminster respecting the deaths of two newly-born children, male and female. The body of the male child was found in the grounds of the Refuge for Adult Females in Vincent Square, and that of the girl in the waste ground in New Victoria Street. The medical evidence proved that the boy had died from strangulation, produced by a ligature round the neck; and that the death of the girl was caused by compression of the nose, and partly from blows on the head. The inquiry was adjourned in order to give the opportunity of obtaining some information upon the subject."

In Hammersmith we find a basket left at the

entrance of St. Peter's School. In this was a child wrapped in a blue serge cloth, by which, according to the surgeon's evidence, it was strangled, and which was absolutely pinned through its skin. In this case, where the delinquent could not be found, a verdict of " Wilful murder" was returned. This is the appropriate verdict in most cases ; and such sound and proper verdicts are likely to do much good by deterring people from the foul deed. But it is strange that such verdicts are usually recorded where the guilty parties are unknown !

At coroner's inquests verdicts of " Wilful murder" are often brought in, only to be quashed at a subsequent inquiry at a higher court. However, at one assizes is recorded the following proper sentence of death for child-murder. At the Cornwall Assizes, on Saturday, before Mr. Baron Channell, Charity Hoskin was found guilty of killing her infant female child by drowning her in the Truro river, and sentenced to suffer the extreme penalty of the law. The jury, however, recommended the culprit to mercy, and the judge, in passing sentence, intimated that the recommendation would be forwarded to the proper quarter.

In Wright's Lane, Kensington, a male child, aged *six weeks*, was left alive and well. "Mr Maydwell said children were being dropped in all directions, and he thought they should offer a reward for the discovery of the parents. Mr. Finch said if they were lukewarm about it they would have more brought to the workhouse." It was then resolved to offer a reward of £2 for the discovery of the parents.

In Hoxton we find a child, in a bundle, floating on the canal water. On Monday, April 1, 1861, the bodies of two newly-born infants were found floating in the Thames, off two of the numerous wharves with which the river is lined. "Ten children," says the *Weekly Register*, "are reported in the last weekly return of the Registrar-general, to have "died from suffocation in bed, *apparently* by accident." Four are returned expressly as " *murdered !*"

Mr. Cox, February, 1862, moved for a return of the verdicts of the juries in coroners' inquests holden during the year 1861 on infants under two years of age. Here is the return taken from the *Daily Telegraph* of April 26.

"*Infanticide in the Metropolis.*—A return of the verdicts of coroners' inquests in the metropolis, on infants under two years of age, during the year 1861, has just been published. It appears that in the eastern division of Middlesex no less than 421 inquests were held, and only in 17 cases a verdict of murder was returned by the jury. In the western division there were 316 inquests, the verdict in the great majority of cases being "Found dead," varied occasionally with a "Found dead in a box." In the city and liberty of Westminster there were 91 inquests; and in the city of London and borough of Southwark, 84. In the metropolitan part of the county of Kent there were 43 inquests; in that under the coroner for the Duchy of Lancaster, comprising a few parishes in Middlesex, there were six inquests; and in that of Surrey 142. The sum total of metropolitan inquests on children under two years of age amounted, therefore, to 1,103 in the course of one single year.

The following Analysis of the Return is given in the *Lancet*.

| Verdicts. | Deaths. |
|---|---|
| Wilful murder . . . . . . . . . | 66 |
| Manslaughter . . . . . . . . . | 5 |
| Found dead . . . . . . . . . | 141 |
| Suffocation; how caused no evidence . | 131 |
| Suffocation; accidental . . . . . . | 147 |
| From neglect, want, cold and exposure, and natural disease . . . . . | 614 |
| | 1104 |

It adds, "It is difficult to analyse these figures

so as to show how many of these children were murdered; probably at least one half of them, and almost as many others may be truly set down as having been secretly put to death under circumstances which did not on the face of them seem to call for an inquest. A large proportion of these children were illegitimate. Between 45,000 and 50,000 illegitimate children are annually born in the United Kingdom."

I think the *Lancet* is considerably in error in forcing one part of the United Kingdom, Ireland, into his statistics. Whether as regards bastardy, or infanticide, Ireland does not deserve to be pilloried with her sister kingdoms. Could anything excuse so heinous a crime as infanticide,—and nothing can,—extreme poverty might do it; but with poverty of the most extreme degree infanticide is happily almost unknown. Let the reason be found out and a lesson taken from it.

The *Daily Telegraph* calculates, from reliable documents, that in a period of five years, from 1856 to 1860, "coroners' inquests were held on the bodies of no less than 3,901 children under two years of age, in London alone." The returns state that of this number 298 verdicts of "Wilful murder" resulted.

In the returns moved for by Lord Raynham,

1857, one clerk says, "I hardly know what is intended by the word *Infanticide*. The return made by the clerk of assize of the Home Circuit for these years is marked "*none.*"

In the Midland Circuit, 1853, Mary Ann Parr had sentence of death passed upon her at Nottingham, but it was commuted to transportation for life. Ann Tommey was indicted for wilful murder at Warwick, 1853; found guilty of manslaughter. The sentence twelve months imprisonment with hard labour. At Lincoln, 1855, Elizabeth Lownd was indicted for wilful murder. She was transported for fifteen years. At Derby, Eliza Beastall was indicted for a similar offence, and was imprisoned with hard labour for two years.

*Northern Circuit.*—Jane Gillie: sentence of death recorded;—punishment, transportation for life.

*Norfolk Circuit.* — One woman sentenced to death;—punishment, transportation for life.

In Lancaster, one indictment; result not stated.

*Oxford Circuit.*—1. Abel Ovens: child, six weeks; sentence, to be hanged; — punishment, transportation for life. 2. Eliza Dore: similar sentence, similar commutation. 3. Mary Robins: ditto, ditto. 4. Sarah Baker: child, two years; ditto, ditto. 5. Maria Tarrant: child, three months; ditto, ditto.

*Western Circuit, Cornwall.* — Richard Jose, jointly with the mother and another person : verdict, manslaughter ; punishment, transportation for life.

*South Wales.*—None.

*Chester and North Wales.*—1852.   Margaret Davies, county Denbigh : convicted of murder ; sentence, death ;—result not stated.

*County of Chester.*—1. Indicted for murder ; conviction, manslaughter ; sentence, seven years transportation.   2. Indicted for murder ; convicted of murder ; sentence, death ;—commuted to transportation for life.   3. Indictment for murder ; convicted of murder ; sentence, death ;—punishment, transportation for life.   4. Same indictment ; same conviction ; same sentence ;—result, transportation. 5. William Jackson : murder of his two children, five and seven years of age ;  same indictment; same conviction ;  same sentence ;—result, hanged.

So in the country.   The crime and the escape of the criminal are equally well marked.   At Liverpool, August 13, 1860, Ann Billington was indicted for the wilful murder of her new-born infant.   The girl denied her pregnancy, but on delivery she placed her child under the cellar-steps, and the surgeon found *a large gaping wound in the throat,* but he could not say that it had " an independent existence or full birth from its mother at the time the wound was inflicted" ( ! ) A verdict of " Concealment of birth" was returned, and a punishment of eighteen months imprisonment, *without* hard labour, was considered sufficient expiation for this murder !

During my remarks on the discussion on Mr. Acton's paper on Illegitimacy, which was read at Liverpool the day after my paper, so surprised was the Rev. Dr. M'Neile of Liverpool, that he interrupted me to request Lord John Russell's permission to put a question to me as to whether there were full grounds for the facts I stated, that children could be killed during their passage from the mother? It was but with too much regret I was able to inform him that not only could such things be done, but that they were frequently done, and not only that, but, to the shame of our jurisprudence be it spoken, *such killing was pronounced not to be murder.* When a gentleman of Dr. M'Neile's great knowledge and position was unaware of this sad fact, we may well infer how little the modes of death resorted to are known to the general public.

With regard, also, to the denial of pregnancy, it is almost incredible under what circumstances women bringing to the world children of shame

F

will assert that they never had cause for pregnancy. I shall give one instance. I was called about ten years ago to see a girl who was suffering from agonising pains. Her sister stood beside me, and after a moment's examination, I told the girl, who seemed particularly sullen and uncommunicative, and who point-blank denied my assertion, that she was pregnant. This expression so shocked the sister, who was recently married, from a feeling of shame at having to meet her husband, that she all but fainted. Owing to this denial I made further examination, and then assured the girl that not only was she pregnant, but that in the course of an hour or two she would be a mother. We begged of her to give some information as to the circumstances of her pregnancy, but she still denied its existence. As labour progressed still did she deny ; and continued this denial while the head was being expelled. When the head was fully in the world I asked if she still denied that she was pregnant, and then, and then only, did she refuse to answer. On the child being wholly expelled, and crying lustily, I asked if she would then acknowledge that she had been pregnant, when she said that she could not then deny it. During the preceding night she was known to have gone several times stealthily to the water-closet, and from the impression made on my mind I watched her narrowly, and did not leave her until I was certain of the child's safety.

On the occasion of this paper of Mr. Acton I dwelt strongly upon the heinousness of the crime of child-murder, and the absurdity of the law as it at present stands as regards punishment; as if any difference existed in the moral turpitude of killing a half-born infant or a full-grown man. In Lord Russell's reply he gave utterance to words which shocked me, as they must have shocked many who then heard and since heard of them, that he did not consider the people of this country were likely to look upon child-murder as they look upon ordinary cases of murder. The enunciation, as quoted in the *Times*, of an opinion that he did not think the law ought to affix capital punishment to the murder of children under a certain age, "say six months," is much to be reprobated, and I only wish I could add that it misrepresents the honest feelings of the country on the subject; but the frequent acquittals in the face of the fullest proof make one fear that some such feeling exists. If it be true, it is a stigma upon a Christian nation. To act up to this doctrine would be to out-Herod Malthus!

Well may the *Medical Times and Gazette* consider this the strangest of all strange things spoken

at that great meeting. Lord John added "that
he could not but think the present punishment
tended to increase what it was meant to prevent,
by leading to acquittals and light punishments."
Surely it is not a very logical inference that because the law proposes a heavy punishment for a
weighty crime, that therefore acquittals and light
punishments must follow, although such has been
the result, as before explained, of laws regarding
infanticide.    There is not, however, the slightest
foundation for the charge in the present instance,
but Lord John Russell, true to his text, will have
it that capital punishment for the *murder* of a
child is a mode of punishment which should be
erased from the statute book.  What next?  What
of the decrepid, worn-out, and fatuous members of
society ?  Are they, too, to be measured according to the state of their mental faculties or bodily
strength ?  I cannot but coincide with the *Medical
Times and Gazette* in considering the avowal of
such opinions " as absurd and immoral ; that such
a scheme is a mad one, and that it is a direct encouragement to infanticide to fix a period to con-
stitute murder."

An ignorant witness at Worcester, the other day,
said she did not know it was wrong to procure abortion ; and well may such an avowal be made when

opinions such as the above are given to the world by our teachers !

But what says the illustrious Percival on the subject, even in an earlier stage of existence, and while the child is in the womb ? "To extinguish the first spark of life is a crime of the same nature both against our Maker and society, as to destroy an infant, a child, or a man; these regular and successive stages of existence being the ordinances of God, subject alone to His divine will, and appointed by sovereign wisdom and goodness, as the exclusive means of preserving the race, and multiplying the enjoyments of mankind." (Percival's *Works*, vol. ii.)

Before I went to Liverpool, in speaking to a friend on whose judgment I placed great reliance, I became quite at issue with him upon the introduction of the moral aspect of the matter into my paper. "Depend upon it," said he, "men will not take your view of it; the public will not consider it their business, and the clergy will be against you to a man." I felt surprised and annoyed that such could possibly be the case, and replied that, come what might, nothing should induce me to swerve from what I considered the proper view. The result proved me right; for in my remarks on Mr. Acton's paper, I said, that as long as we took the merely temporal view of the question we began at the wrong end, and should never succeed. As long as we based our laws upon offences against the state, instead of crimes against the Almighty, we were in error. That were this latter and more proper view taken, things might be rendered comparatively easy, and that here our best police must be found amongst the clergy. Let them bring up their young flock in the fear of offending God, in respect to this as well as to other crimes, and the other police force would have less to do. This met with a welcome response, and I was gratified throughout this sitting to find the moral and religious aspect of this question the one most generally considered.

Mr. Joseph Kay, on the *Social Condition and Education of the People*, says, "The existence of the 'burial clubs' is one of the most fertile sources of infant mortality." His chapter headed, "The Frightful Extent of Infanticide amongst the Poor," shows children neglected for sake of the burial money; and that parents promise to pay their debts when a certain member of the family—generally a child—should die ! A servant, whose child was ill, refused medical assistance from a lady, saying, "Never mind, it is in two burial clubs !" Even hired nurses have been known to speculate on the lives of infants committed to their care. (This he says on the authority of a burial club official.) Two young women proposed to enter a child in a club and to pay alternately. On inquiry as to the relationship, it was found that *the infant was placed at nurse with the mother of one of the young women.*

At Manchester, August 1858, William Coulters, aged *eight years*, was cruelly murdered by his mother. The poor boy was an idiot, and illegitimate. He was found nicely laid out in bed, and quite cold, with his throat cut. This the mother admitted she did with a razor. Her husband was in Australia, but she was receiving the addresses of some old man, and expected shortly to be married to him. Hence her motives. The jury returned a verdict of " *Wilful murder ;*" but what the subsequent trial resulted in I do not know.

At Lewes, July 1858, Emma Sutton, a good-looking girl, aged 15, was indicted for concealing the birth of her child, having been originally committed upon a charge of wilful murder. As usual in such cases, the judge, Mr. Justice Willes, charged the grand jury that the medical evidence did not "*in a sufficiently positive manner*" establish the fact that the child was born alive. Therefore the trial for concealment. She denied her pregnancy, but on a certain day she was seen going towards the scullery carrying something which had the appearance of an infant.  On search being made, the body of a female child was found, with a piece of tape—one of the prisoner's garters—*tied tightly* round its neck.  Six months hard labour absolved her !

At Ipswich a girl is tried for concealment.  She denied her pregnancy, and acted with much coolness and cunning.  She was delivered of an infant, which her sister found in a drawer in their common bed-room, its throat being *cut from ear to ear* with some blunt instrument.  The sister told the girl's father, who called to the prisoner, " Good God, Jane ! what have you done?"  The girl *then* " fell down as if shot," and remained speechless and unconscious for many weeks.  Lord Campbell directed the jury to acquit the prisoner, as " there could be no concealment on her part if she were unconscious !"  The girl was *perfectly conscious when she coolly and cunningly did the deed*, coming down to rejoin her sister at work after the murder was committed.  It was when *upbraided* with it that she was *struck down ;* and yet such were Lord Campbell's directions.  The jury, " evidently nothing loth," at once said, " ' Not guilty,' my Lord," a result which was hailed with acclamation by a crowded court.  Never was there a greater perversion of justice !  Happy judge, who, without even an attempt to show unconsciousness at the time of the murder, so charged the jury! Complaisant jury, who, "nothing loth," without an attempt to prove the girl unconscious *when she killed her child*, delivered, in face of their *oath* to find according to evidence, a verdict diametrically opposed to evidence!

At Reading occurred the melancholy case of Mary Newell, who, when brutally repulsed by her seducer, and refused aid of any kind, went at midnight, and having attached a bag of stones around her infant's body, threw it into the river. She was little above twenty years old. The magistrate's office was surrounded by a mob who hissed the prisoner as she was conveyed to goal. Her seducer, Francis, was afterwards properly subjected to the roughest and most ignominious treatment by the men of Reading, and had to decamp from the town. This unfortunate girl was convicted of murder, but the sentence has been commuted to that of penal servitude for life.

So at Pershore in Worcestershire, and in Worcester itself. So at Hambledon, near Godalming, where Mary Jones, aged 19, who always denied her pregnancy, cut her infant's throat with a knife. She was found guilty of wilful murder, and Mr. Baron Martin, in passing sentence, gave expression to the fact that offences of that character were un-happily very prevalent. So in Warwickshire, where an old woman of 82, and her granddaughter, aged 22, half burned, and then strangled the child of the latter.

So at Derby (1860?), where a woman was charged with the murder of her daughter's child. According to the evidence of one surgeon, death must have resulted from the cord being cut, and criminally left untied; according to the evidence of another, from the skull being fractured, suffocation at last ensuing from the child being buried alive. Here there was conflicting evidence, and the wo-man was acquitted.

At the Bedford Assizes, March 1855, Elizabeth Lound, aged 18 years, was sentenced to fourteen years transportation for the wilful murder of her illegitimate child, born on the 24th of August pre-viously. On the 1st of September she left the workhouse, and on her way to her brother's she "*actually buried the child alive,*" placing it on the ground and covering it with loose earth and sods!

From the *Registrar-General's Weekly Returns,* April 1858, we find six deaths by suffocation, all except one being infants. In a "Weekly Return" for August 1860, we see five deaths, of which four were those of infants, and these were referred to murder or manslaughter. But from these isolated examples let us go to more general conclusions, and see what the average of ascertained infanticides is in a given five years. In doing so we cannot fail to be struck with the numerous other cases of a most suspicious character, quite bearing out the expressions of Mr. Wakley.

In the nineteenth *Annual Report of the Registrar-General*, we have the statistics, such as they can be given, of infanticide in England for the five years, 1852-56. But, in fact, such is the state of the law, and so rarely does conviction follow child-murder, that an approximate idea only can be given of the number of infanticides.

The above report gives for the five years—

| | |
|---|---|
| Infanticides . . . . | 608 |
| But there are of Overlaying - . | 530 |
| Suffocated by food, under 5 years of age - | 129 |
| „ Bed-clothes „ . - | 905 |
| Manner not stated, or other- } under 1 year | 936 |
| wise than the above causes under 5 years | 137 |
| Strangled, under 1 year - . . | 49 |
| „ under 3 years - . . | 3 |
| Hanged (!) under 1 year* - . . | 5 |
| „ under 3 years - . . | 1 |

The Registrar-general says "the causes of suffocation were not stated in nearly half the cases."

---

* We have in future to add *decapitation* as one of the modes of death.

Then we have a return of poisoned under one year,—by opium, 52 ; by laudanum, 172 ; By Godfrey's cordial, 74. There are murders of children under one year, manner not stated, 15.

Many of the deaths under these heads must be looked upon, to say the least, with considerable suspicion, but the "cause of death" returned precludes us from saying positively that foul play existed. Again is the expression of Mr. Wakley called to mind (page 19), that 300 deaths by infanticide take place annually in London, although many are returned as dying from other causes—such as "Still-born," "Overlaid," etc., etc.

What is the meaning of "Injury at birth"?—is it, for instance, anything like the following, just now given in the *West London Observer;* where Hannah Cook was remanded before Mr. Ingham with having caused the death of her illegitimate child? One medical gentleman proved "that it was possible that the injuries the child had received might have been caused by the unskilful delivery of the prisoner." Another was of opinion that the "injuries were too extensive to have caused death in that way, and that they were the result of considerable violence." Well might he be of that opinion; for a third gentleman, called in to the *post-mortem* examination, found a "*frac-*

*ture of the skull, a fracture of the arm, a fracture of the jaw, and a laceration of the right corner of the mouth !"* Truly, if this be " injury at birth," and not " infanticide," in the Registrar-General's next report, the soundness of the conclusion may well be questioned.

The state of the law as regards still-born children leads to great abuse, and, indeed, to great crime. There is no registration of the deaths of still-born children, so that in fact a child may be made away with and then buried as a still-born child without any further question. On September 15, 1859, an inquest was held on an infant in the parish of St. Pancras. The surgeon of the work-house deposed that there were in the dead-house the bodies of *seven* dead children, which it was alleged were still-born. Two of them he believed were born alive. The coroner said that he had no doubt but that the grave-yards of the metropolis teemed with hundreds upon hundreds, he might say thousands of murdered children, and that infants had no protection. He believed it to be the same over the entire kingdom. At a meeting of the guardians of Marylebone, Dr. Bachhoffner said he believed this statement of Mr. Wakley to be under the mark ; and that at present the production of a paper signed by almost any body, insured

interment on payment of half-a-crown. While at
press I learn that the Home Office has offered a
reward of £150 for the discovery of the persons
guilty of several recent infanticides in Marylebone.

At a meeting of the directors and guardians of
the poor of the parish of St. Luke, Chelsea, held
October 1859, the attention of the board was called
to the question of the disposal of *still-born* children. Mr. Livingstone desired to know if any
means could be discovered how these children met
with their deaths, as the master's report assisted
to prove the fact asserted by Mr. Wakley, the coroner, in regard to wholesale child murders. He
thought it was of vast importance that a close scru-
tiny should take place into all such deaths.

The coroner for Middlesex observed (1859),
"That he felt surprised that such a number of still-
born children should be sent to the different workhouses in the metropolis, and without any investigation buried in the coffins of adult paupers.
When that was done could there be any wonder at
all of the number of child-murders reported from
time to time? He should attribute it to carelessness, in the want of some proper authority
having a check upon the burial of such children."
From the 1st of January to the end of November,
the *Medical Times and Gazette* says, "Ninety-

three still-born children had been thus brought to the workhouse, Marylebone, for interment ; and in some instances there was so much doubt about the case, that the assistant overseer had refused to receive the child."

In his address on Public Health at Liverpool in the Social Science Meeting, 1858, Lord Shaftesbury stated that " no less than 60,000 ' *still-born* ' children are produced in this country every year !"

Mr. Wakley considers that in London alone 200 infanticides yearly escape detection.

At a subsequent meeting of the guardians of Marylebone, Dr. Bachhoffner, after describing the magnitude of this question—illegitimate births and dry-nursing—" stated that the Earl of Shaftesbury, if he was informed correctly, would allude to it in a lecture at Bradford next week. In the five years ending December 1858, there had been registered the births of 1,109* illegitimate children in this workhouse, and it was a lamentable fact that the number of legitimates were only 271, and that out of this 1,109, there were 516 deaths, or about 46 per cent. In St. Mary's district there were registered 582 births against 109 deaths, giving a per centage of $18\frac{8}{10}$. In All

---

* It is subsequently stated that this number had been *registered* in the district, 821 of which had been born in the workhouse.

Souls' district the births were 145 against 87 deaths, or about 53 per cent. In St. Mary's district, in which Queen Charlotte's Hospital was situated, he had given the number of births as 582, and though it was said that unmarried women were not admitted, he thought he might fairly state that nearly 400 out of that number were illegitimate. In the Christ Church district there were 223 births, against 209 deaths, or about $93\frac{7}{10}$ per cent. In St. John's 148 births against 129 deaths—this district showed the greatest amount of deaths in comparison with the return of births—which he believed was caused by a greater number being placed out to what was termed dry-nurse. In Cavendish Square district—which many would consider a moral one—the number of births registered were 40 against 36 deaths. This showed a frightful state of mortality, if even something worse was not going on."

Here then we have evidence how wide-spread is the crime of infanticide, how keenly the pulse of the nation beats to its existence, and how general is the conviction of its increase. Is there a remedy? and if so what is the nature of that remedy? are questions which must now occupy every mind. The country is on its trial before the civilised world, and most ardently may it be hoped that the issue of that trial may be favourable, and that men will not be found to fold their arms in listlessness, or shut their ears in despair, while the sickening wail of murdered children appeals to the better feelings, and seems to prompt them to exertion.

Under the old law a woman could "swear a child" on any person she wished. Under the altered law "corroborative evidence" is required; and certainly something was necessary to correct the abuses formerly existing. But at the same time too much should not be required of women at present, and protection should be given more especially where cases of heartless seduction have taken place. In such cases the wealthy but heartless seducer should not be allowed to trample his already victim in the mire by putting into requisition the resources of his well-filled purse, and by employing all the legal force he can command to baffle and weary out the poor struggling creature that he has ruined for life. Cases of this kind have occurred, where appeals being made from the magistrate's decision to a higher court, the poor applicant finds herself lost and confused,—in some cases, perhaps, forsaken by the solicitor in whom she trusted,—who throws up her case for REASONS HE BEST KNOWS; and so in her absence loses both character and claim. Girls in such miserable

G

plight are much to be pitied, and their case well deserves to be taken up by the philanthropic and the charitable.

Mr. Kendall, M.P. for East Cornwall, obtained a return from which it appears that summonses in bastardy to the amount of 157,485 were issued in the fifteen years from 1845 to 1859, both years inclusive; of these, 124,218 were heard, and of these, orders for maintenance were issued in 107,776 cases; 15,981 cases being dismissed, which, together with the cases that did not come on for hearing, make 49,709. In this great number of cases the woman had to struggle with her load of grief and shame;—chained to the cold earth, down, down, to rise no more.

At a meeting of the *Law Amendment Society*, where, by the way, my published ideas were freely made use of, without acknowledgment, it was contended that as it lay in the power of a woman to prevent seduction, she should not be at liberty to recover money for an offence to which she was a consenting party! This doctrine shows small appreciation of the working of the human passions, or the weakness of the human heart. If the man were as liable to become pregnant as the woman, then it might apply, but not otherwise. When cool reason succeeds bewildering passion, the woman finds that all the consequences of the momentary crime are fastened on her, the man walks off unscathed.

The crime of infanticide being acknowledged as universal, the question arises what are the best means to get rid of it. Like the crime itself, any proposition for its amelioration seems surrounded with difficulties. Let us see what has been formerly attempted, with the results; and should we find that foregone efforts have succeeded, and that modern improvement can offer nothing better to our view, does it not follow, as a matter of logical sequence, that we should adopt the means that have been successful, rather than acquiesce in the frequency of the deed?

After considerable attention to the subject, with all the draw-backs to their usefulness, I am still inclined to think that foundling hospitals, properly managed, hold out the most promising results, and would conduce much to the prevention of the crime of infanticide. But in this kingdom there may be, indeed is, a strong feeling against such institutions. It has been said that they are not according to the "genius" of the country. But is infanticide according to the "genius" of the country? Few, it may be hoped, will reply in the affirmative. Then, if it be not, let *some means* be taken to stop its havoc. What happens to be according or not according to the genius of a country seems sad nonsense. Many things which have been pronounced according to the genius of this country, as the slave trade of former times, etc., have met a reversal; and other things which were pronounced *not* according to this "genius," such as reform, free trade, etc., seem to thrive very well.

Hanging for slight offences seemed at one time pretty much according to the "genius" of the country, but the fashion is now happily exploded; and crinoline, which our more scantily-robed ancestors could never have been persuaded to be according to the "genius" of the place, bids fair, risk to life and limb to the contrary notwithstanding, to become an "institution" of the country. Indeed, there is much of fashion in all these things, and even the broad-brimmed Quaker gives way to its influence.

I cannot agree with the *Edinburgh Review*, vol. xxxviii, p. 440, that foundling hospitals "may safely be termed a great public nuisance, leading to unchaste life and to child-murder beyond any other invention of the perverted wit of man." This, however, is often the style in which they are written of in this country, but the charges are without foundation; and to mal-administration may be traced many of the evils of such institutions, rather than to any vice inherent in the system. Were the charges correct we should expect the philanthropists of other countries, who so warmly support these institutions at once to fall away and shun them as more evil than the crime they are supposed to prevent. But we find no such desire on the part of the founders and supporters of those places, and amongst their supporters history shows us some of the greatest benefactors of mankind ;— some whose singlemindedness and purity of intention has never, by any section of the people, been called in question.

Indeed, the table given at page 34, and the conclusions there laboriously arrived at, would seem to settle that question, and to prove that where foundling hospitals could lead to such results, there must be some peculiarities in the social condition of the people to account for them. Certainly, the fact seems established by the paper, provided only the statistics be correct, that more unchastity exists where foundling hospitals are unknown, than in places where they form an institution. That *infanticide* is more rife in such places scarcely requires an affirmation.

From the investigations of the Baron de Gerando it appears that the illegitimate births are more

than the average, *only in four of twelve departments* in which foundlings are most numerous.
The opposite is shown in twelve departments in
which the number of foundlings is smallest, and
where two only exhibit illegitimacy in less than
its average form.

Indeed, if the editor of the *Edinburgh Review*
had had the opportunity, which we enjoy, of seeing
the returns of the Registrar-General of Scotland
for one of the quarters of 1858, he must have considerably modified his opinions and expressions.
Illegitimacy is unhappily rife enough where foundling hospitals do not exist, and even amongst ourselves. The following statistics are given in the
*Lancet*, 1858 :—

" *Illegitimacy in Scotland.*—The returns of the
Registrar-General of Scotland show that the counties in his list in which the proportion of illegitimate births is greatest are not those which are
rapidly advancing in population, or which contain
our largest cities, with their overcrowded inhabitants, but are rather those which are more purely
agricultural. Thus, in Scotland, the counties of
Renfrew and Lanark, with their teeming population, shows only 6·1 and 6·7 per cent. respectively
of illegitimate births; Linlithgow 6·7 per cent.,
and Edinburgh 8·7 per cent. ; while the proportion

of illegitimate births rises to 11·1 per cent. in Peebles, to 11·6 per cent. in Roxburgh, to 12·5 per cent. in Selkirk, to 13·1 per cent. in Kincardine, to 14 per cent. in Kirkcudbright, to 15·7 per cent. in Dumfries, to 16·2 per cent. in Aberdeen,* to 17·1 per cent. in Banff, and to the enormous proportion of 17·5 per cent. of the births in Nairn. The general comparison of the social condition of Scotland in this respect with other nations around us does not afford as favourable a result to the land of John Knox as might have been expected, especially when the facilities afforded by Gretna Green are remembered. It appears that in Sweden only about 6·5 per cent. of the births are illegitimate ; in Norway, 6·6 per cent. ; in England, 6·7 per cent. ; in Belgium, 6·7 per cent. ; in France, 7·1 per cent. ; in Prussia, 7·1 per cent. ; in Denmark, 9·3 per cent. ; in Hanover, 9·8 per cent. ; while in Austria 11·3 per cent. of the births are illegitimate."

So as to localities. In some parts of England illegitimate births occur in a much higher ratio than they do in others. "In the Isle of Portland or in the neighbourhood of some of the collieries, a girl's pregnancy is merely a preliminary step to her marriage ; while in other places such an occur-

---

* In Aberdeen, one child in seven, or more than 14 per cent., is said to be illegitimate.

rence would ruin her character and blight her hopes."* Indeed, it is well known that, in some quarters, where the female is disinclined to yield to the solicitations of the man, one of the most successful arguments on the side of the latter is, that should pregnancy result he will marry her. And this promise is considered binding, and generally fulfilled. Thus we have "in five counties more than 9 in 100 children born out of wedlock: Cumberland, 10·5, and Westmorland, 10·5; Norfolk, 10·3; Shropshire, 9·4, and Herefordshire, 9·3; while in Kent it is 5·9; Huntingdon, 5·6; Devon, 5·6; Cornwall, 5·1; Stafford, 5·8; Warwick, 5·7; Durham, 5·4; Monmouth, 5.3. In *moral* London, where, according to the police reports, hundreds of finely-dressed prostitutes can muster in *one* building near Leicester Square during a single night, the proportion of bastard children registered is only 4·2, or 3·2 in another calculation. Well may Dr. Farr consider this figure as understated, and that "in the large towns it is probable that the children born out of wedlock are not registered to the same extent as other children." (*Registrar-General's Nineteenth Report.*)

In the same way we cannot judge of the mo-

---

* British and Foreign Review, April 1842.

rality of different cities from the number of illegitimate children born in them. For instance, it would not answer to take Paris and Vienna, in the foundling hospitals of which so many illegitimate children are received from all quarters and from all distances, and compare them with London where no foundling hospital exists. It is to the given illegitimacy of entire countries we must look. Thus Dr. John Webster says that more illegitimates than legitimates are born in Munich; that in Vienna half the children born are illegitimate; and that in Madrid one in five is in the same position; while Paris supplies one illegitimate birth in every four born.

The dictum of the *Edinburgh* is further controverted as regards child-murder, or the next thing to it, the desertion of children, by tables giving the number of illegitimate births and the number of foundlings in a certain number of departments in France. It will be observed that in the first six the foundlings amount to 3,550 in 3,577 illegitimate births; while, in five others, they amount only to 366 in 8,118 cases. So that we cannot in these latter departments for a moment assert that any inducements which foundling hospitals offer for the desertion of children have been taken advantage of; and in the former, foundlings, including legitimates, are less in number than the illegitimate births. The statistics of these latter departments more especially show that it is not to want of chastity that the desertion of children can be traced as a cause.

| Departments. | Date. | No. of Illegit. Births. | Found- lings. |
|---|---|---|---|
| Bouches du Rhone    -    | 1832 | 1219 | 825 |
| Charente Inférieur    -    | 1824 | 582 | 573 |
| Corsica    -    -    -    | 1824 | 141 | 143 |
| Cher -    -    -    -    | 1827 | 391 | 411 |
| „    -    -    -    -    | 1828 | 354 | 377 |
| Dordogne -    -    -    | 1829 | 578 | 755 |
| Ille et Villaine    -    -    | 1832 | 312 | 466 |

The following table gives an opposite result :—

| | | | |
|---|---|---|---|
| Jura -    -    -    -    | 1826 | 588 | 68 |
| „    -    -    -    -    | 1828 | 452 | 58 |
| Moselle    -    -    „    | 1824 | 720 | 78 |
| Haut Rhin    -    -    | 1826 | 1221 | 34 |
| „    „    -    -    -    | 1832 | 980 | 78 |
| Seine et Oise    -    -    | 1826 | 822 | 30 |
| Haute Saone    -    -    | 1824 | 1060 | 8 |
| „    „    -    -    | 1829 | 1434 | 9 |
| „    „    -    -    | 1831 | 841 | 3 |

Further, we shall find that, in the ten years there were born in France, 9,031,908 legitimate children, and 703,663 illegitimate ; while only 336,281 foundlings and deserted children were admitted into the hospitals—many of these being, as a matter of course, children born in wedlock. Prosperity or adversity will have much to do with the desertion of children, independent of the state of morality existing ; and in years when people are stinted in their means of living, or in times of actual famine, the number of deserted children is certain to increase. This has been noticed in Belgium in that year of terrible pressure, 1817, where the number of foundlings rose from 3,000 to 3,945. During the same year there was an increase of 800 in the number of foundlings in Paris alone ; and throughout France of 5,000. This is an abuse that could scarcely exist in this country if foundling hospitals were established, as the workhouses would afford a vent for the pressure. The same places must always tend to lighten the expenses attendant on foundling hospitals ; whereas, on the continent, where poor laws do not exist, all the expenses fall directly on the state, or on the contributions of the charitable.

In the *three* winter months of 1803, when poverty pressed hard on the Parisians, one half of the entire admissions of the year took place ; the greatest number being deserted in the last of the three months when the means of the poor were exhausted. This cannot, however, be cited as a general rule ; and, as in cases where the most intense sense of shame cannot make the ruined mother abandon her illegitimate offspring ; so, as shown by MM. Terme and Monfalcon, poverty will not lead to desertion. Severe distress existed in Lyons in 1836, but this did not lead to parents abandoning their children,—especially those newly-born. Poverty, indeed, seems rather to influence parents in abandoning children some years of age than newly-born ones.

It is melancholy to reflect that in the ancient days of Rome, many who took to their homes the poor children that their parents made outcasts, did so from a most sordid self-interest, as they often put out their eyes or maimed them in different ways, in order that by exhibiting them in this condition they might induce the charitable to give them money.*

With very different feelings did those who instituted foundling hospitals go to work. Their sole object—men and women—seemed to be to put a stop to infanticide, and by throwing the mantle of charity and secrecy over the fallen woman, and showing, by pointing out a mode of support for her child, that her whole prospects in life were not to be ruined by having a dead weight upon her

---

* Even Seneca vindicated the maiming of children on the ground of their being slaves. Justinian, A.D. 530, prohibited the slavery of these unhappy ones.

exertions, they took away, once and for ever, the greatest incentives to infanticide. As in the conducting of every other institution for the amelioration of human suffering, it was impossible that such institutions should not be abused. They were abused, and in consequence reformations of various kinds and at different times were had recourse to, and even suppressions were tried, until it was found that infanticides increased in consequence.

In the very infancy of Christianity institutions were founded for the support of foundlings, and this is a significant fact. The Emperor Justinian gave his full support to them. A foundling hospital was established at Milan as early as the year 787; and one was founded, at least for orphans, in Constantinople, in 1096, by Alexius I. In 1198, Innocent III allotted part of the hospital of Spirito Santo at Rome for the reception of foundlings, in order to prevent infanticide. Austria, Spain, Russia, Belgium, etc., have many such institutions. In France they exist in greater numbers than in any other country, and great care has been bestowed upon them, as well by those who founded them and cultivated them from feelings of pure and absolute charity from the period of 1204, when Guy of Montpellier instituted one, to the time when Napoleon looked to them as a training ground for soldiers to replenish his army, and placed them under the protection of the state in 1789. At one period, as mentioned, they were suppressed in consequence of abuses; and in the reign of Louis XIII, the prevalence of infanticide caused a pious woman, Madame Legras, to institute an asylum for outcasts.

The times of the Crusades—of which the present civilization of Europe, owing to the opportunities for interchange of ideas, is in a great degree the result—amongst many other stirring and beneficent incidents, gave rise to the Orders of Hospitallers, the duty of some of whom it was to visit and relieve the poor and sick, and to provide for orphans and foundlings. One of the Orders especially, that of the Holy Ghost, consisting chiefly of lay-members, devoted themselves most assiduously to the care of foundlings. This brotherhood was incorporated in 1204 by the Pope, and Guy of Montpellier was nominated master of the hospital of *Santo Spirito*, which was restored by Innocent. Voluntary contributions from all parts of Christendom went to the support of this hospital, and institutions of this Order were to be found numerously scattered throughout Europe. Succeeding Popes were great benefactors to this house. Numerous abuses crept into these institutions, leading to their great injury, and even to their suppression, to the great detriment of the foundlings, and to the decided increase of infanticide. The church was unable to afford the necessary funds; and all charitable institutions were utterly destroyed during the wars of the League. Foundlings were placed at the door of the cathedral of Nôtre Dame, and a clergyman standing by begged for contributions for their support from the charitable as they passed. So things remained until the time of St. Vincent de Paul, when children might be found dead or dying in the streets and byways, or floating on the Seine. I have been told by a late medical officer to one of the largest workhouses of London, St. Pancras, that the mortality, by infanticide, in that quarter would be frightful, were it not for the facilities offered for the reception of the outcast mothers.

The hospital of *San Spirito* itself, the oldest of the Roman hospitals now existing, is said to have been founded, for the relief of his countrymen, by a Saxon king, who went to reside at Rome in 728. It is desirable to learn how it is conducted at the present day, and with what effect as to the rearing of children and the prevention of infanticide. We get some particulars concerning these matters in a recent work, *Rome and its Ruler.*

Children are sent to this institution not only from Rome and its neighbourhood, but from the most distant provinces, and even from neighbouring states. About 900 are thus received yearly, part of the hospital being laid aside for the reception of deserted children, and part for the *re-reception* of children sent to the country to be nursed. About two-thirds of these children are illegitimate; the remaining third are legitimate, and the children of people too poor to support them. Where a family has more children than can be supported, one is committed to the "wheel," and taken into the hospital. The same holds good where a woman dies in childbed, and the father feels his efforts hampered by the child. The delicacy of the mother or the child is another cause, as well as where the mother has no nourishment, and cannot afford a nurse; or where the child is of an infirm, strumous, or rickety constitution from birth. In such cases, the food bestowed at the hospital is often sought for. But in some cases parents, able but unwilling to support their children, their cupidity or laziness getting the better of their natural feelings, take advantage of the charity intended for far different purposes; and hence arises one of the abuses of such institutions, owing chiefly to the indiscriminate mode of admission which the turning boxes afford to the unworthy. Those whose intention it is to prove the identity of their children, in order to claim them at some future time, may take various precautions for that purpose.

In the Roman States, all incentives to infanticide are thus removed; while the children are much better cared for, and have much more chance of surviving than they could have in the homes of their parents, where poverty is but too often extreme. These children are taken great care of, and are soon sent into the country for the benefit of the purer atmosphere. The mortality of late years has been said not to exceed ten per cent. In the *Quarterly Review* (vol. x, p. 241), the writer says, "the praises bestowed by travellers on the Italian hospitals are justly due to such noble institutions, and the regulations observed with respect to the reception of foundlings are far better calculated to prevent the horrid crime of infanticide than those practised in our country. We sincerely wish that the Governors of the Foundling Hospital would condescend to borrow a few useful hints from a people who are supposed to have carried their charitable establishments to the highest degree of perfection."

The hospital of *San Rocco*, which is connected with the Foundling Hospital, was devoted in 1770,

H

by Clement XIV, exclusively as a lying-in-hospital,
where unfortunate women may be confined, and
through which disgrace may be prevented to families.   The occupant of any bed is perfectly protected from the curiosity of that of the neighbouring one.   The females are received without question being made, and may even veil their faces
in order to avoid recognition.   They can leave the
hospital on their recovery, without any prying eye
seeking to fathom their secret.   The annual number of admissions, about 1841, is stated by Mori-
chini to be for ten years, 165.   The nurses take
great care of the children left to their charge.
They are well paid and fed, and well looked after
by the Sisters of Charity.   Yet pain, and feeble-
ness, and sickness, are to be traced, as may
be well imagined, on the faces of many of the
infants.   The name and origin of the child will
be taken down, if the person bringing it so wish,
but under seal of secresy.   The child may thus
be identified in aftertimes, if any claim be made
to have it restored.   The nurseries consist of
three rooms: two for the healthy, and one for the
sick children.   In giving these children out to
nurse, every care is taken that the nurse is in good
condition; that her milk is not too old.   Every
precaution against imposition is also taken; such,

for instance, as a woman applying for her own child, and thus being paid for suckling it.

Paris, at the time of St. Vincent de Paul, contained about 1,000,000 of inhabitants of every condition of life; from that of the highest opulence, to that of the most abject misery. Virtue and vice jostled each other; exalted purity and daring libertinism could alike be found. Owing to this extreme poverty and this rampant libertinism, many children were sacrificed as soon as they were born. The churches and public places were selected for exposure of infants. They were taken away, by order of the police, and left with a widow and her two servants, in Saint Laudri Street. This woman had not means sufficient to support them, and they were often suffered to die through want. Even the servants, in order to be relieved from their cries, gave them medicine to put them to sleep,—often the sleep of death. In this respect, it is to be feared, that they are imitated by nurses and mothers of the present time. The children were even sold for so low a sum as twenty sous to any person who chose to buy them, and as charity had little to do with the purchase, speedy death was the result. M. Collet, in his *Life of St. Vincent de Paul*, says that children were killed for magical operations, or in order to afford baths to those who considered such a horrible process conducive to longevity.

Horrified at this state of things, St. Vincent de Paul beseeched some pious ladies to go to Saint Laudri Street, and see if something could not be done. These ladies were terrified at the magnitude of the sight,—at the multitude of abandoned children. They could not possibly provide for all,— they would for some. They therefore drew lots for twelve, and procured a house, at the gate of Saint Victor, for them. Madame Le Gras, with some Sisters of Charity, took care of them. The difference between those children, thus cared for, and those left at Saint Laudri, was so quickly apparent, that pity was excited for the latter, and a general meeting was held in 1640. St. Vincent placed before Ann of Austria the sad state of affairs, and this lady, who was said to consider that day as lost on which she had not done some good deed, obtained from the king the revenues of five large farms, amounting to 12,000 livres. But state troubles increased, as did also the number of foundlings, the support of whom exceeded 40,000 livres ; and the ladies of charity at once declared they could no longer bear the enormous expense.

In 1648, another assembly was convened, and a general determination was evoked, to continue what was considered so good a work. The king granted the château of Bicétre, designed by Louis XIII for invalid soldiers, and here certain of the children were conveyed. The air being considered too keen for the children, two houses were purchased in Paris, the first stone of the church of one being laid by the Queen Mother. To these, Louis XIV contributed most liberally; but it was found that 150,000 livres were necessary to the support of the children. The cause of these outcasts at this time became most critical;.any delay would have been fatal to it. Civil war, famine, and its necessary attendant, disease, prevailed. The barricades which were erected in Paris, and the violence which existed, made the Queen resolve to starve out the city; and the Court therefore left, with the minister, Cardinal Mazarin, for St. Germain-en-Laye.

Despite of all exertions, however, it was not until ten years had elapsed after the death of St. Vincent de Paul, which took place in September 1660, that the *Hospice des Enfans Trouvés* was recognised as one of the Parisian hospitals. From all parts of France children were sent to this hospital, and many like it were quickly founded in the provinces. Frequent altercations arose among the authorities as to the duty of providing for those children ; but after the Revolution of 1789, the law became the protector of them throughout France, and ordered houses to be opened for their reception. Many difficulties were in the way, as well of a financial character, as in the fact of the Sisters of Charity having been driven away, and with them the best friends of the outcasts :— women who gave up all ease and worldly prospects in order to carry on a work of benevolence. Napoleon recalled these, and rapidly instituted provisions for the relief and support of foundlings. And here again it may be noticed, how often selfishness may aid or retard works of charity. The Emperor, in order to carry on his wars, made ample provision for those outcasts, with whom, in a few years, he hoped to replenish his army. He also established, by the '*Tour*,' an indiscriminate and secret admission. Many remonstrances against this system were made throughout the provinces, but ineffectually. He even assumed the power, but never acted on it, of placing the children at the disposal of the Minister of Marine on attaining their twelfth year.

One of the greatest evils connected with these institutions, as observed by Remacle and more than acquiesced in by Gaillard, is undoubtedly the system of secret admission which is supplied by the turning boxes. The facilities afforded by these for depositing children, offers temptations to unworthy married people which they too often take advantage of; and it has been calculated that the number of legitimate children deserted in Paris amounts to 1 in 10, and even to 1 in 5 in some parts of France. These numbers, however, may not be accurate, as many children are left at the hospital without a certificate to show whether they are legitimate or otherwise. Terme and Monfalcon estimate the number of children born in wedlock yearly deserted by their parents at 2,400. This happens more especially in large manufacturing districts. In other places, as is well attested, it is only extreme want that forces married parents to the unnatural deed of deserting their children. Lyons furnishes proof that many married women confined at the *Hotel Dieu*, there endeavour, and often succeed in the attempt, to leave their children at the hospital.

This sort of thing, indeed, led to that great abuse of the London Foundling Hospital, and was in some degree the means of diverting its well-meant charity from its original purpose, until it at last deteriorated into what it is now — a mere orphanage—utterly useless in preventing a single case of infanticide. In the first year of indiscri-

minate admission, according to Mr. Brownlow's
*History of the Hospital*, 3,296 children were received ; in the second year, 4,085 ; and in the ten
months of the third year, during which the system
was continued, 3,324. These were brought from
all parts of the country, and by tricks, one should
think, easily detected. In a town 300 miles distant a woman traded in these poor children, and
carried them, assisted by her two daughters, at so
much a head. These poor infants often suffered,
as in the continental instances, from foul play. A
person was tried at Monmouth for the murder of
his child, " which was found drowned with a stone
about its neck." The father had paid a travelling
tinker a guinea to carry it to London, and this
person murdered it.

Another case appeared, says Mr. Brownlow,
where a man having care of five children in baskets, got drunk, and slept on a common all night.
In the morning he found three of the five children dead. In another case, seven out of eight
infants sent from the country in a waggon died
before they reached London. The mother of the
surviving child followed on foot and occasionally nourished, and so saved it. These are but
some of the abuses which could be easily stopped.
Here it may be observed that a large number of

these children must have been the offspring of married but unnatural parents.

Another great abuse arose from the fact that the parish officers "emptied their workhouses of the infant poor, and transferred them to this general sanctuary provided by government." This is an abuse which at the present time could also be soon remedied.

The *cash account* for 1860 shows receipts to the amount of £13,272 15s., and for this great outlay 37 children are yearly admitted, while there are 206 applications. The many rejected, says Mr. Brownlow, are so on account of want of funds. Thus, in fact, the *principle* of foreign foundling hospitals is admitted, but funds are wanting to open the portals more widely. Something more might be added, that in foreign hospitals the embracing of the outcasts is a labour of love, but that here it entails an array of well-paid officials. The number of children at present supported from infancy to the age of 15 is 460.

"With its revenue," says Mr. Acton, "of the present value of £11,000 a year, and with an assumed income, within the present century (according to the statements of the charity commissioners) of £40,000 a year, this institution so wanders from its legitimate path, and from propriety of adminis-

tration that each of its inmates costs it nearly
£360 before attaining 15 years of age, besides
being unhealthily and unnecessarily reared in the
atmosphere of the metropolis, and having a poor
start in life after all."

"In considering the question of mortality," says
Mr. Brownlow, speaking of the present time, "the
children of the hospital should be classed under two
heads, namely: First, those under the age of three
years in the *country;* and secondly, those from
three to fifteen in London." We might expect, after
this, some particulars of the mortality at the present
time, but none whatever are given! However, we
find that, while in 1859 there were 505 "children
remaining" at the expense of the hospital, there
were only 12 deaths!

The *tour* consists of a cradle placed in a wall
between two doors, one of which on being opened
causes a bell to ring, which immediately informs
the attendant that a child has been left; or a box
turning on a pivot in which the child can be placed
and notice given; and these offer facilities for admission which cannot be too strongly reprobated;
and yet it is surprising to find in France so many
warmly espousing this form of admission. The
absolute mystery with which this mode shrouds
the transaction, by which detection is rendered

impossible, recommends it to those who desire that no chance shall be given for unkind and harassing reproaches towards the unfortunate mother; and as the most effectual means of preventing the crime of infanticide. On the other hand, those who see the yearly number of foundlings undiminished, view this mode of admission most unfavourably, and endeavour by a modified and wiser system to meet the difficulty as to infanticide, while it opens to the really unfortunate female an asylum to hide her shame.

The advocates for the *tours*, however, assert that the partial suppression of them has been followed by many more infanticides than usual. But the data they go upon are not quite trustworthy, and the murders may be attributed to other causes. They also assert that the suppression has not been followed by any diminution in the number of foundlings, but both statements cannot be correct; as if there were a greater number of infanticides, and also a greater number of foundlings in a given time than before, it could only have occurred by more births having taken place. The advocates for the suppression of the *tours* show that where 24 departments had suppressed 48 *tours*, infanticide increased in nine only in a given time; while in 13. it was less, remaining unchanged in two.

The experiment was tried in other departments, and the result certainly does not show an increase of infanticide.

By a table given by *Remacle* it appears that more infanticides occurred in proportion in a given time in places having a greater, than in those having a lesser number of *tours*. A table is also given showing the average of infanticides in countries with, and in countries without *tours*. The average is in the former 1 in 351,321 inhabitants; and in the latter (a doubt being expressed about Prussia, where the number of infanticides appears unusually large, 1 in 76,873), as 1 in 426,861. The countries given are France, Belgium (Brabant, etc.), and Ireland, where *tours* existed; and England, Belgium (Liege, etc.), Grand Duchy of Baden, and Prussia, without them. In some provinces of Belgium the closure of the turning-boxes has not been followed by increase of infanticide. The result of the suppression in France is stated to be different; and it appears that while in three years previous to its introduction 82 cases of infanticide were sent for trial, in the three years subsequently the number increased to 117.

Another great objection to the indiscriminate admission afforded by the *tours*, in addition to what has been already noticed, is, that children have been brought from almost incredible distances, and that there are people who make a trade of carrying these children to the hospitals, often utterly careless whether they reach them alive; and, indeed, it is wholly impossible in many cases, owing to the length of the journey in the glowing heat of summer or the chilling cold of winter, that these weakly little ones can survive. It has even been proved that the mercenary carriers got rid of their trouble by murder. It was ascertained that those children brought from a greater distance than 50 miles to the Dublin Foundling Hospital died there; 48 per cent. only being the average of the other children. So with those children who were probably brought from a distance and deposited in the *tour* of Poictiers. The mortality of these is remarkable when compared with that of those removed to the hospice from the Maternité; and especially shows how fatally cold must act during the transit of the children from the place of their birth to the hospital. In summer 7 per cent. of the former die to six of the latter; while in *winter* the proportion is as 19 to 10.

Another great cause of mortality amongst infants is the almost insuperable difficulty of finding a substitute for mother's milk, and the abuses that frequently occur from the employment of an insufficient number—from the difficulty of procuring them—of nurses, or nurses whose milk is too old, and therefore unfit for a newly-born child. Regarding nurses, who can wonder at the great mortality of the Dublin Hospital, when informed by Mr. Wakefield, that two infants were frequently put to one woman, and even as many as five! Deaths to the amount of 37 per cent. within a fortnight after admission were the natural result of this state of things, or 72 per cent. of all the deaths during the residence of the children. In Madrid three children are often put to one woman, and the result, according to MM. Terme and Monfalcon, is pretty similar.

No substitute has yet been found for the natural milk of the mother. This has been fully exemplified by the following statistics. At Parthenay a mortality under one year of 35 per cent. took place. About the same figure, or a little higher, was shown at Poictiers. At X——, 80 per cent. died by the time they reached one year of age. In all these places every possible care and attention is paid to the children, but in the last locality all are hand-fed, and to this only can be traced the great mortality. Every possible effort was made, unsuccessfully, to reduce this havoc, and recourse was obliged to be had to suckling. A child who

is suckled by a good nurse while in a hospital has
some disadvantages when transferred to some poor
and badly-fed nurse in the country, as it is the
poorer classes only who receive these children, and
some of these are often at the same time suckling
a child of their own; but removal from the atmosphere of an hospital and country air must make
up for much of this.

The facts deduced by M. Villermé from a comparison of three localities where different systems
of feeding are pursued, show fully how superior
suckling is to all the forms of feeding. He instances Lyons, Rheims, and Paris. All are suckled
at Lyons; at Rheims all are hand-fed, the children
usually remaining in hospital one or two days; at
Paris the children are usually though not invariably suckled, and remain in the hospital much
longer. The result is shown in the mortality being
at Lyons, 33·7; at Paris, 50·3; and at Rheims
60·9 per cent.; so that the rapid removal from
hospital at Rheims fails to make up for the unnatural system of hand-feeding. And yet this sojourn,
as at Paris, is one of the most fruitful sources of
mortality, as there are some diseases absolutely
traceable to the aggregation of children, and peculiar to foundling hospitals themselves. Of these,
one, *"l'endurcissement du tissue cellulaire,"* is

only to be met with in such institutions. *Muguet*, an apthous ulceration of the mouth and fauces, is another form of disease which attacks and rapidly destroys these poor outcasts, and many affections become complicated with a form of pneumonia of a very fatal character. This shows the absolute necessity of making the stay of infants at these hospitals as short as possible; and well was this understood at Lyons, and so promptly acted on, that not more than 20 children were found in its large hospital at the time of a visitation. The experience of Sir Hans Sloane in 1741 of the London Foundling Hospital, showed in round numbers a mortality amongst the suckled and the dry-nursed of 20 and 54 per cent. respectively.

Another circumstance accounting for the favourable results of the system pursued at Lyons is the great care observed as to the mode of carriage in the removal of the children. Children, often weakly and always delicate, are easily affected by circumstances of transition, and every possible precaution is requisite to their safety. The children, well and comfortably wrapped up, and placed in cradles, are carried on the heads of the persons sent with them. This is considered the best mode of conveyance, and to a different and less careful mode adopted in Paris, has been attributed much of the mortality of infants there.

Here, again, as to both these instances, we are reminded of the early days of our own Foundling Hospital, when people traded in this carriage of children and brought them from all parts of the country. The extended frontiers of France also enabled people of other countries to send their children to the French hospices, and thus might be found in that of Lyons, children from Valois, Fribourg, Geneva, and Savoy.

Regarding the mortality at the London Hospital, when first opened, Mr. Brownlow says, " that many received at the gates did not live to be carried into the wards ; and this although the nurses 'were under the superintendence of certain ladies—sisters of charity.' Of 14,934 received, only 4,400 lived to be apprenticed out, being a mortality of more than 70 per cent." Considering that the apprenticing out must be at a pretty ripe age this does not seem so overwhelming a mortality.

In the efforts of St. Vincent de Paul it will be remembered that there were no *"tours"* or turning-boxes to receive infants indiscriminately ; and it may be re-asserted that the facilities for concealment given by such were above all others the causes of those abuses which militated so much

I

against hospitals for foundlings. However desirable it may be, and however noble the thought must be allowed to have been, which prompted charitable people to throw the cloak of compassion and concealment over the fallen woman; still the unchecked license to deposit children at will cannot well help leading to demoralisation which a better conducted system of registration would prevent. All credit must be given to those who, with the dread of a wide-spread infanticide before their eyes, were willing to try any chance rather than systematic *murder* should stain their country and offend the Deity. The profound mystery which shrouded every circumstance connected with the turning-boxes, and the guarantee given by them to those who might have sinned, and then become horror-stricken at their position; and at the ruin of character as well as the destruction of family happiness which its discovery must be attended with, made this mode of admission be warmly espoused by many. Lamartine calls it an "ingenious invention of Christian charity, which has hands to receive, but neither eyes to see, nor tongue to tell."

About 25 years ago the laws connected with foundling hospitals created considerable attention in France. How to make provision for, and to check the number of illegitimate children, seemed the great problem. With this view prizes were offered by different societies, and amongst the essays, the most successful in the treatment of the subject may be mentioned those of MM. Terme and Monfalcon, M. Remacle, and the Abbé Gaillard. The two first named wrote *An Historical Account of the Statistics and Moral Condition of Foundlings ; to which are added a Hundred Tables*, Paris and Lyons, 1837. The third sent in an essay *On Foundling Hospitals in Europe, and principally in France, from their origin to the present day*, Paris, 1838 ; and the Abbé Gaillard contributed *Researches into the Statistics and Moral Condition of Foundlings, Illegitimate Children and Orphans, and the Laws respecting them in France, and in many other countries of Europe*, Paris, 1837.

These works were ably analyzed, and much matter added, in the *British and Foreign Medical Review* for April 1842 ; and the tables are so clearly given, and the abstract matter so ably discussed, and so fully brought within compass, that advantage has been taken of placing the article fully under contribution. At the same time, it must be observed, there are some apparent inconsistencies.

While warmly admitting, for instance, that "it was a noble thought to cover the sins and frailties of the weak or the wicked with the mantle of charity, and to obviate the consequences of those vices which religion was not strong enough to root out," the writer says that, in his belief, public opinion in England has declared rightly against such institutions. He yet denies, in the end, the assertion that they have never done good, and that they are incapable of being turned to good account. He considers the foundling hospitals in France are undergoing the changes which the times call for, and that "these changes are being effected by men of great wisdom and benevolence;" that these men have done great good, and are likely to do much more, and that their undertaking is by no means a hopeless one. He especially recommends, —a recommendation quite as necessary now as in 1842—the works above mentioned "to all who fancy there are certain stereotyped forms according to which charity must needs work, and who deem it impossible that mankind can ever be benefited except by the adoption of their theories, and the employment of their remedies."

The fear of a growing deterioration of morals in the increase of illegitimate children,—an increase in some respects only apparent, and to be accounted for by increase of population—as well as the great expenditure of eleven millions of francs, caused the inquiry, above alluded to, to be made. And this was the more necessary, as the mortality continued as great as in former times, nearly 60 per cent. of the children dying within the first year of their birth. Attention was firmly rivetted on the progressive increase of children at the public charge. This increase was only apparent; as the statistics of the earlier period could not be relied upon, and indeed no record was kept before 1789. In 1784, the number was considered by M. Necker to be 40,000, and gradually increasing it amounted, in the year 1833, to 129,669. In the former period, the hospitals were supported by private charity, by the church, or by occasional grants of the sovereign, and the public had no claim on them; at the latter period, they were institutions of the country, regularly established, and to which the public had a right.

Previous to 1824, there was no record of the number of exposed children, as compared with the births throughout the entire of France; and the account now given is of a period of ten years,—from 1824 to 1833. The following is the conclusion arrived at—

FOR THE FIRST FIVE YEARS.

1 Illegitimate birth to 13·85 total births.
1 Child abandoned to 29·7      do.
1   „        „        to  2·15 illegitimate births.


FOR THE LAST FIVE YEARS.

1 Illegitimate birth to 13·83 total births.
1 Child abandoned to 28·22      do.
1   „        „        to  2.04 illegitimate births.

We see here, during ten years, little difference; and it is said that the previous thirty years point to the same conclusion.

The above-mentioned authors considered that the proportion of illegitimate children was much greater at the time they wrote than at the beginning of the century, the estimate being 1 in 20 at the earlier period, to 1 in 13 or 14, or 7 per cent., at the present. This at first sight might appear unfavourable to the morality of the French; but the reviewer very fairly and very satisfactorily shows that this should not be the case; and that the facts can be accounted for by "the Conscriptions, which drained France of its young men during the first ten or twelve years of the nineteenth century, and which would sufficiently account for the small proportion of illegitimate children, when compared with the numbers presented in after years." And besides, there were other sources of error, which prevents the documents brought forward being entitled to reliance.

A system which offers no difficulty of admission, the *bureau ouvert*, has long been practised in Paris; and many able men, and some of the prize essayists already mentioned, recommend this plan for adoption in France generally. At the same time that this system has been adopted in Paris, the *tour is open*, but it is seldom used, so unclogged by difficulties is the former. It was proposed that these should be multiplied throughout France; and that every facility should be given by them to girls in the unhappy position of being the mothers of bastard children, to leave their hapless burthens in safety. In Paris, the child could be left, the name and address of the applicant being simply given. The chief magistrate of any locality would be the only person cognizant of the circumstance, and strict secresy is enjoined. How different is this from the repulsive plan adopted at the London Foundling, where a poor girl is bound to appear, in order to be examined, before a board of male governors.

In the Maternité at Paris, like the hospital of the Holy Ghost at Rome, strict secresy is observed as to the person who is there confined; and the same secresy it was proposed to extend to the hapless mothers of bastard children throughout the empire. This secresy would answer all the ends sought, and it would be a guarantee that the institutions should not be abused either by worthless parents sending their children to them; or by a trade being driven by bringing children from distances necessarily fatal; or the injustice being committed of having neighbouring countries send their spurious offspring across their frontiers, to be reared at the expense of people of a different kingdom.

It was also proposed to give private relief to poor women,—women who might otherwise abandon their children,—in order to enable them to bring them up at their own homes. Much good has resulted from this plan, as well as from that of exacting a promise from all confined at the Maternité that they should suckle their infants while in the place, and take them with them when going. To use the words of the *Review* :—" In the course of the first eight months after the adoption of these measures, the mothers of 458 children have been induced, by kind persuasions and by some pecuniary assistance, to retain their infants whom they had intended to abandon. One of the most gratifying features, too, in the working of this system is, that the deaths among the infants, whom their mothers were persuaded to keep charge of, amounted to only one in fourteen, while the mortality among the foundlings was one in three." These plans had been tried fourteen years, when the Baron de Gerando gave the following result :—

"The year 1838, when compared with the seven preceding years, has yielded the following results :—

|  | Mean of the seven former years. | Year 1838 |
|---|---|---|
| Children admitted - - - - - - - | 4,929 | 3,037 |
| Died in the hospice - - - - - - | 1,306 | 763 |
| Sent to the country - - - - - - | 3,651 | 2,277 |
| Claimed by their relations - - - - | 39 | 28 |

"During the course of the same year, 1838, although the *tour* has remained constantly open, the number of children deposited in it has not exceeded 60. The number of children exposed in the public thoroughfares, during the course of the year, was 28 ; and the number of children deserted in the entries of houses or in the interior was 11." The data collected in their Maternité, during the seven years prior to 1838, compared with those of 1838, have given the following results :—

|  |  | Mean of the seven former years. | Year 1838. |
|---|---|---|---|
| Women | admitted - - - - | 2,960 | 3,153 |
|  | delivered - - - - | 2,642 | 2,946 |
| Children of Women delivered in the Maternité. | still-born - - - - | 144 | 144 |
|  | died in the hospice - | 72 | 119 |
|  | retained by their mothers - - - - - | 717 | 1,437 |
|  | abandoned by their mothers in the hospital | 1,751 | 1,297 |

" Thus two-fifths of those children, who would probably have been abandoned to public charity, if the government had not taken steps for applying those regulations which are sanctioned by law, have by these measures been preserved to their mothers and families."

This was a great improvement ; expenses were lessened, and infanticides and desertions were not increased. And all this took place, too, while indiscriminate admission, through the *tour* which remained open, was still accessible.

It also shows that no substitute, not even the milk of another woman, can be found for "mother's milk" ; although, when this cannot be had, that of a wet-nurse, properly chosen, affords beyond all others the best form of nutriment. To find a well-adapted form of food for children, irrespective of wet-nurses, would be a great desideratum, for, as is well remarked by Mrs. William Baines, when a woman goes out to nurse, while the adopted child reaps the benefit, her own child must suffer the loss by having to be brought up by hand. Another consideration is, that when women go out to nurse their husbands' comforts are not attended to, and thus temptations offer to wean a man from home and to contract irregular habits.

Another great objection in the minds of many to

foundling hospitals is that the mortality is so great in these institutions ; and it is argued, because so many children perish by a certain period, that therefore these hospitals have failed in preserving life. It is unfortunately too true that the mortality in foundling hospitals has been very great, but I consider this is altogether beside the question. The matter simply comes to this. Murder of children is being committed in a country, and hospitals are instituted in order to prevent this crime ; but owing to circumstances in some degree inseparable, perhaps, from such places ; and from certain diseases which seem to follow where children are crowded together, a frightful mortality ensues. But see the difference. In one case, the most frightful of crimes is being perpetrated ; in the other, every effort that human ingenuity can compass is brought into requisition, but fails in preserving life. In one case, a human being is wantonly deprived of the life which God had given, and the murderer walks abroad ; in the other, the oil and wine which the Good Samaritan pours into the wounds of the infant traveller is ineffectual in its object, and the child dies ; but can any one for a moment compare the murderer as he walks away affrighted from his deed of blood, with the Samaritan who takes a last sad look at the expiring infant whose life he tried to save?

An argument against foundling hospitals based upon the great mortality of the children left in them, might be a fair argument in the statistics of heathen nations. The "saving of life" might come well enough from them. So low an argument can scarcely be creditable to a Christian people, whose paramount cause of action in such cases should be the "prevention of murder." Lord John Russell must have been thinking more of heathen than of Christian morality when he put forward the detestable doctrine that the punishment of death should follow infanticide only in cases where the child attained a certain age! It only required impunity to be extended to the murderers of the crippled and the weak in order to render the parallel perfect with the conduct of the inhabitants of ancient Greece, the Thebans excepted.

Fearful indeed has been the mortality in foundling hospitals, but much has been done, and much can still be done, to lessen this; and in showing forth this mortality it is not right to compare it with that of the public generally. The unfortunate infants are taken into such places under most unfavourable circumstances,—often almost dead when they are left. Brought forth under circumstances of want, grief, and shame, a comparsson as to mortality should only be made between them and the children of the poorest localities, where pestilence and misery claim their victims early ; and then the statistics, although still most unfavourable, could not appear so wholly so as they now do. It is not right to bring into the calculation any portion of those children of the wealthy and well-to-do, who have every aid the world can afford in warding off disease and strengthening their rickety frames. How many of these poor children, with mothers circumstanced as their's were, if they escaped the knife or the cord, would be likely to succumb before the first year of their birth, is a question which should imperatively demand to be taken into consideration.

The mortality in different countries, as well as in different localities, must also be taken into account in noticing that of different foundling hospitals. For while in England, according to the *Second Report* of the Registrar-general, the mortality for children under one year is 14·6 per cent. ; in Russia generally it is 27 and in some districts 31.

Let it be noticed, also, how great is the mortality in hospitals and poor-houses where the destitute are taken in—and these we must always have for our unfortunate fellow-subjects ; — foundling hospitals without their good intentions or merits. In speaking of the workhouses of Marylebone and

St. George's, Mr. Acton says, that "out of 392 illegitimate children that died in 1857, the large proportion of 362 died before they were one year old." From the records of the workhouses of Marylebone, St. Pancras, and St. George, although the exact proportion of deaths could not be ascertained, yet it was shown that "nearly half the illegitimate children of these parishes died," or 392 out of 877 births before their first year. Let those who declaim thoughtlessly against foundling hospitals think of this.

Still it is right to repeat the fact, were it only for the purpose of inciting to an improved *hygiene*, that the mortality in foundling institutions has been most lamentable, at the same time that care and an improved system has led, and may still lead, to far different results. Beckman considered that eleven-thirteenths of all the foundlings in Paris in 1790 and 1800 perished annually through hunger and neglect. This is very different to the statement of Chateauneuf, who says that the mortality in Paris at the close of the last century was 80 per cent. or four-fifths; and that in 1824 this was reduced to 57·6. In 1789, in the Foundling Hospital of Vienna, 54 died out of 100 in the hospital. It is said that even in favourable years there is a mortality of 70 per cent. The year 1811 was very fatal to the children. The Emperor Joseph II took great interest in the hospital, frequently visiting it, and at one time instituted an inquiry how far different kinds of diet might influence the mortality. The result still showed a sad waste of infant life, and in 1813 the plan more particularly adopted in Italy was tried; and the hospital was permitted to be merely a depôt for children until they could be removed to the country, to the care of nurses there provided. The result of this change appeared in 1822, when instead of one in two, *the deaths had diminished to one in four and a half, or nearly 22¼ per cent.*

Great care is bestowed on the Foundling Hospitals at St. Petersburgh and Moscow, but yet the mortality is very unfavourable. In 1811, out of 2,517 admitted, 1,038 died. In 1812, out of 2,699 admitted, 1,348 died, or not quite 50 per cent. In the province of Archangel, 377 died in 1812, out of 417 admitted. At Palermo, in 1823, 429 died out of 597 admitted. At Metz it was calculated that seven-eighths of the children died. The mortality in the Dublin Foundling Hospital, as before noticed, was still more grievous. In

* Dr. Bisset Hawkins's *Elements of American Statistics,* quoted by Dr. Beck.

Berlin a fourth part survived, and there they had
the advantage of being suckled by their mothers
who were confined in the *Charité.*

"At *Grenoble,* of every 100 received, 25 died in
the first year; at *Lyons,* 36; at *Rochelle,* 50; at
*Munich,* 57; and at *Montpellier,* even 60. At
*Cassel,* only 10 out of 741 lived 14 years. In
*Rouen,* one in 27 reached manhood; but half of
these in so miserable a state that, of 108, only two
could be added to the useful population. In *Vienna,*
notwithstanding the princely income of the hospital, scarcely one in 19 is preserved. In *St. Petersburg,* under the most admirable management
and vigilant attention of the Empress Dowager,
1,200 die annually out of 3,650 received. In
*Moscow,* with every possible advantage, out of
37,607 admitted in the course of 20 years, only
1,020 were sent out."*

It need scarcely here be pointed out how very
different is the account here given by this journal
to that of Hawkins, quoted by Beck as above,
where, under an improved system an average of
one death occurs in four and a half admissions.
This, instead of one in 19, would show $14\frac{3}{4}$ lives
preserved in 19, and points out the danger and
impropriety in statistics of being biassed by pre-

* *Edinburgh Medical and Surgical Journal,* vol. p. 321.

judice and preconceived opinions. The average at the London Foundling Hospital of those that died under one year during 10 years was *one in six*, or 16⅔ per cent., and in subsequent years even less than this. This is a most favourable return.*

Again, glance at the results of the improved methods adopted in different localities, and it must be admitted that one great objection to foundling hospitals,—their excessive mortality,—should be much modified. Take Lyons, as one of the best examples. From 1822 to 1831, a period in which remarkable improvements were carried on, the mortality of children at the hospital was (including the still-born) only 1 in 11·3, and from 1831 to 1836, when the working of the institution was more perfect, only 1 in 12·39, whereas from 1802 to 1810 the mortality was 1 in 7·4. In 1820, the mortality was 50 per cent. In later years it has come down to 30 per cent. Here is a most gratifying saving of infant life; and the percentage is more favourable in still more recent times.

So as regards localities, the researches of M. Villermé show that in the most fashionable part of the city of Paris, the deaths of infants under one year amount to 17 per cent. of the total deaths;

---

* Highmore's *History of the Public Charities in and near London* : Rees's *Cyclopedia*, Art. *Hospital*.

K

while in one of the poorest districts, the 12th arrondissement, they reach 25, and in the still poorer locality of the Rue Mouffetard, 32 per cent. Even in the 12th arrondissement, it is important to notice that streets not occupied by poor persons, the Rue St. Honoré and the Rue du Roule, have a mortality, under one year, of only 14 per cent. of the total deaths; and that the mortality from birth to the age of twelve months, in the Rue Mouffetard, is equal to that from birth to ten years in the Rue St. Honoré and Rue du Roule."

Now look for a moment at the mortality in London for the last quarter of 1861. In the *eastern district*, the mortality of children under five years was *fifty per cent.* of all the deaths; in the western, thirty-six. This shows what may be due to local influences. In the eastern district, there are 266 persons to an acre; in the western, 200; in the city, 105. Even in the whole metropolis with its great, but unequally divided, wealth and comforts, and with thirty-six souls to the acre, the mortality bordered on 42 per cent. Surely, we must look at home a little, where such a state of things, in the words of the *Lancet*, "continues to be a great stain on the honour, and a heavy burden on the conscience, of the nation."

Density of population, poverty and ignorance,

must ever be conducive to a high mortality amongst children. It is in places where these exist, and where the outdoor occupations of mothers lead to the neglect and drugging of children, we may look for a disproportionate number of deaths :—indirect infanticide very often, and direct infanticide, too, from the drugging system. The result of ignorance, as bearing on infanticide, is particularly shown by the fact that of 810 persons tried in a given time, in France, for this crime, 697 could neither read nor write.

Some remarks will be necessary on an analogous crime, and one that there is no doubt is but too frequently committed. This crime is "abortion"; and is constituted by the expulsion of the contents of the uterus by a certain period of pregnancy. That period is fixed in this country before the twenty-eighth week ; that which occurs subsequently being called "premature labour." Continental authors have a different arrangement. The seventh month also marks an epoch at which a fœtus is more likely to be viable, as few live that are born before that period. Still, far as this object is concerned, it might be better to name the sixth month, because the fœtus may then be *born alive* although not generally *viable.* Indeed, even at *a very early period* of pregnancy, the

fœtus when aborted may show signs of life by
movements of the limbs, etc. Not that the law
makes any distinction of this sort, as the term
abortion applies to the expulsion of the fœtus at
any period of pregnancy, and in this sense it is
equivalent to the term miscarriage.

The law makes the attempt to procure abortion
punishable as felony (1 Vict., c. lxxxv, s. 6). It
enacts that, "Whosoever, with the intent to procure the miscarriage of any woman, shall unlawfully administer to her, or cause to be taken by
her, any poison or noxious thing, or shall unlawfully use any instrument or other means whatsoever, with the like intent, shall be guilty of felony,
and being convicted thereof, shall be liable, at the
discretion of the court, to be transported beyond
the seas for the term of his or her natural life, or
for any term not less than fifteen years, or to be
imprisoned for any term not exceeding three years."

By this law, capital punishment, which formerly
existed and depended upon the senseless distinction whether the woman had " quickened " or not,
was abolished. What with the uncertainty attending the earlier periods of pregnancy, and the doubts
as to her real situation which must always exist in
the mind of the female, abortion is seldom attempted
before the third month, and as the signs become

more unequivocal after the fourth month, the crime is perhaps oftener attempted between that time and the fifth month than at any other.

There exists a doubt whether, under the above law, a woman is liable to punishment who affects abortion *in her own person;* but it does not require even the consent, or a request on the side of the female, in order to render criminal the attempt on the part of another. The crime it is said would never be attempted without the consent of the mother, and that therefore to admit such consent as a sufficient defence would be to render the law inoperative and void. The *intent* must appear on the face of the pleadings, with which any means may have been put into requisition in order to cause abortion ; and this can generally be judged by an accurate inquiry into the means employed. If instruments have been used with this object, their nature and the description of injuries inflicted, as well as the other consequences of their employment, will usually allow of a proper judgment being formed ; and if drugs have been employed their nature must be ascertained in order to know whether they come under the head of " noxious "; for unless this be proved no conviction can follow. At the same time that the drug must be shown to be of a " noxious " nature, it is not necessary to conviction that it should be attended with the result sought after—that of procuring abortion —or that even the woman should be injured. A difference of opinion may arise as to the noxious or harmless nature of the drug employed, and much in such case will depend on the quantity administered, as well as on the circumstances under which, and the frequency with which, it is given. Many medicines in certain doses may be quite harmless, which in larger doses may become injurious. Such may be said of savin and rue, which act as irritant poisons when given in large doses, or small ones often repeated.* The same may be said of aloes, cantharides, and other medicines, as to their abuse in quantity or frequency in the case of pregnant females. This has been shown at a trial (Reg. v. Stroud) at the Abingdon Summer Assizes, 1846. Dr. Taylor† alludes to the fact that the quantity of the substance taken does not affect the question, provided the dose be frequently repeated. He mentions a case tried at Exeter Winter Assizes, 1844, in which Mr. Reynolds was examined. The prisoner prescribed two powders, each weighing one dram—one consisted of colocynth, the other of gamboge, and with them was mixed half-an-ounce

---

* *Ann. d'Hygiène*, 1838, ii, p. 180.

† *Med. Jurisprudence*, p. 490.

of balsam of copaiba. They were to be mixed, and a fourth part taken every morning. In answer to the question whether such a mixture was noxious or injurious, Mr. Reynolds very properly said that each dose would be an active purgative and might thereby tend to procure abortion. That one dose might not be productive of mischief in a healthy countrywoman, but its frequent repetition might lead to serious consequences.

Sarah Whisker was tried at the Norwich Lent Assizes, 1858, for administering to the prosecutrix some powdered white hellebore for the purpose of procuring abortion. A medical witness said he considered hellebore a noxious drug, but that as he did not know of any case in which it caused death he did not consider himself justified in calling it a poison! Perhaps if the drug had been arsenic this witness might have been in a position to make a similar answer. Another medical witness said that in his opinion hellebore belonged to the class of poisons. It is strange that a doubt could exist in the mind of any medical man as to hellebore being a powerful irritant poison, as it is well known to have caused death in many instances; yet this witness, while he admitted the drug to be " noxious to the system," hesitated as to its being poisonous! It has been observed, even in small doses, to cause convulsions and even death ;* and in fact took its name from its destructive properties—"because it destroys life if eaten."† The judge in summing up said, *that* was to be regarded as poisonous which was commonly understood to be so, and that the evidence was sufficient to bring hellebore within the meaning of the statute. The person was found guilty,‡ and though abortion did not ensue, as the woman had been guilty of several acts of a like kind, she was transported for life.

The law was formerly more severe in those cases; for by a statute of James§ (21 Jac. c. 27), *concealment* of the birth of a bastard child was made conclusive evidence of murder, unless the woman could prove the child was born dead. The extreme harshness of this law defeated its object, and could not be allowed to continue ; and the 43 Geo. III, allowed the jury to find that the prisoner had concealed the birth of the child; but here, in order to punish for the concealment, a bill must be found for the murder,—an unpleasant predicament for the grand jury. This last statute enacted, " If any person shall willingly, maliciously,

---

* Duncan's *Edinburgh Dispensatory*, p. 270.

† 'Ελλεβορος: παρα το τηβορα ελλειν.

‡ *Medical Gazette*, xxxvii, p. 830.

§ Amos's *Lectures on Medical Jurisprudence, Med. Gazette,* p. 738.

and unlawfully administer to, or cause to be administered to, or taken by any of his majesty's subjects, any deadly poison or other noxious or destructive substance or thing, with intent thereby to cause and procure the miscarriage of any woman then being '*quick*' with child, the person so offending, his councillors, aiders and abettors, knowing of and privy to such offence, are felons, and shall suffer death as in cases of felony, without benefit of clergy. And if any person shall wilfully and maliciously administer to, or cause to be administered to or taken by any woman, any medicine, drug, or other substance or thing whatsoever; or shall use or employ, or cause or procure to be used or employed, any instrument or other means whatsoever; with intent thereby to cause or procure the miscarriage of any woman, not being proved to be then quick with child, such person and such his councillors, aiders and abettors, are guilty of felony, and liable to be fined, imprisoned, and set in the pillory, publicly or privately whipped, or to suffer one or more of the said punishments, or to be transported for any term not exceeding fourteen years, at the discretion of the court before which they are tried and convicted."

Under the first section, proof should be given that the woman was quick with child when the party was indicted under it; but under the second section it was not necessary to prove even pregnancy, the *intent* to procure abortion on the part of the accused being all that was desired. It does not appear necessary to prove that the means used were such as would be necessary to procure abortion in ordinary cases, (R. *v.* Phillips, 3 c. 74 N. P.), so that it can be shown that the accused considered she was pregnant. This was the first statute ever passed to this effect. By Lord Lansdowne's Act, the woman could be proceeded against for the concealment simply (9 Geo. IV, c. 31). This Act contained most extraordinary, almost incredible provisions; as, if the woman were *quick with child*, there was no offence committed by using instruments to procure abortion; but provided the woman was *not* quick with child and that instruments were used, then it was held that the offence was committed and came within the meaning of the statute. This inconsistent statute was, however, remedied.* Even in the construction of the remedied Act, as in the former, it was held that to the charge, which is not capital, it will be an answer, that the woman was not *pregnant.* For either the minor or capital offence it was not necessary to prove the drug was calculated to *pro-*

---

* See Russell on *Crime*, Addenda, p. xxxvi.

*cure abortion*, only that it was given with that intent; though in the prosecution for the capital charge it must be proved that the medicine given was a poison, or of a noxious and destructive nature.*

The distinction which existed in the English law as to the punishment respectively if the woman were or were not "quick" with child, and which was abolished as mentioned already by the 1st Victoria, c. 85, sect. 6, was condemned both by foreign jurists and the medical authorities of our own country.† A woman was said to be "quick" with child when she felt the motions of the fœtus *in utero*,—a most preposterous definition; and in the case of R. *v.* Phillips, it was decided that when a woman swore that she had *not felt the child alive* within her, she was not to be considered *quick with child*, according to the meaning of that Act.

With regard to *intent*, a case is recorded where a jury acquitted the prisoner on the ground that he had given a harmless medicine to the woman, as she threatened otherwise to destroy herself in order to hide her shame; and I am cognizant of some cases where application was made for the purpose of procuring abortion, and where the in-

---

* Amos.
† Paris and Fonblanque : see also Beck's *Med. Jurisprudence.*

dignant medical man gave some tonics, and then, a month or more having elapsed, the female was threatened with being brought before a magistrate if at a given time a child were not forthcoming. By means such as this the criminal intentions of women might be frustrated; still, this conscientious proceeding on the part of a medical man might not always be unattended by danger, as in case of any legal investigation, his name might be brought up as having attended and prescribed for a person in the pregnant state, who might admit the object for which she consulted him, and the information which she imparted to him. Indeed, this has been done in order to extort money in California, and in consequence the legislature there, at the instance of the Medical Society, decreed that the person upon whom abortion is practised, shall be held as guilty as the abortionist.

The design of this law is thus explained by the *San Francisco Medical Press*:—"The design was to prevent wicked female adventurers from attempting to blackmail medical men by applying to them, even when not pregnant at all, for the ostensible purpose of having an abortion produced, but who, when the doctor would, in order to get rid of them, prescribe some inert substance, would have a prosecution commenced against him for producing a criminal abortion, and cause much trouble, unless he would buy them off in the beginning. Or, what is still worse and entirely unavoidable on the practitioner's part, they could swear him guilty of producing criminal abortion when he had not even been applied to at all in the matter. This occurred once in this city; and although the perjury soon became apparent in the case, still the idea of a respectable medical man being arraigned as a criminal is not very palatable, even though it ultimately becomes plain to everybody that his prosecution is based upon perjury alone. As the law now is, the practitioner has only to perform his duty conscientiously to be free from this species of annoyance; while these wicked adventurers, under the assumed connexion of dear husband and wife, will have to conduct themselves cautiously, or otherwise find a quick way to the States' prison."

The reason of the distinction as to quickening, and the laws founded upon it, arose from the dicta of the old philosophers, handed down as they have been to the present day, that life is imparted at a certain period to the foetus *in utero*. The obsequiousness with which the dogmatic opinions of those philosophers were followed by most of the governments of the world is remarkable.

According to Plutarch, the stoics* considered that the soul was united to the body during the act of respiration, and not before. Hippocrates† considered that the male fœtus became animated 30 days after conception, while 42 days elapsed before animation took place in the female; that the fœtus is animated when perfectly formed. Galen‡ believed animation occurred 40 days after conception. Aristotle considered a masculine fœtus to be animated on the fortieth, and a female on the eightieth day after conception. Pliny takes the same view, and on the authority of these illustrious men, but more particularly "propter auctoritatem doctissimi Hippocratis," many laws were passed in the reigns of Antoninus, Adrian, and Aurelius, in which abortion was rendered criminal only when induced after the fortieth day; the embryo not being believed to be endued with life before that period. It need scarcely be said how mischievous must have been the influence of such opinions.§ The doctrine of the stoics gave way in the reigns of Antoninus and Severus to that of the Academy; that life was imparted to the fœtus

---

* Plutarch's *Morals*, vol. iii, p. 230, London.
† *Lib. de Nat. Puer.* Numb. 10.
‡ *Opera Galeni de usu Part.* lib. xv, cap. 5.
§ Le Clerc's *History of Physic*, vol. i, p. 19.

at a certain period.    Theologians in the Church of Rome* made a distinction between the inanimate and the animated fœtus to which the soul is added by the creation of God, and adopted the opinions of some of the old philosophers, more particularly those of Aristotle, as to animation in the male and female, but the canon law altogether negatived the doctrine of the stoics, for Innocent II condemned the following proposition :—" It seems probable that the fœtus does not possess a rational soul as long as it is in the womb, and only begins to possess it when born, and consequently in no abortion is homicide committed."    Sextus V† inflicted severe penalties for the crime of abortion at any period ; these were in some degree mitigated by Gregory XIV, who, however, still held that those procuring the abortion of an animate fœtus should be subject to them, viz., an excommunication reserved to the bishop, and also an "irregularity" reserved to the Pope himself for absolution.‡

As long, therefore, as the gender was not known the penalty was computed from the eightieth day, when even the female was presumed to become

---

* *Theologia Moralis,* concin. A. F. P. Kenrick, Philadelph., 1841, vol. i.

† *Constitutione Effrænatam*

‡ *Constitutione sædes Apostolicæ,* anno 1591.

animate. But while allowing this distinction the canon law pronounced abortion even of the inanimate fœtus " a grievous sin which cannot on any account be extenuated, as it prevents the life of man who is to be." Innocent II condemned the proposition ;—" It is lawful to procure abortion before the animation of the fœtus, lest the girl, being discovered pregnant, might be killed or defamed." So amongst the Fathers. Tertullian* says homicide is prohibited even while the blood is chosen into the man, or deliberates as it were about the sex; (" dum adhuc sanguis in hominem delibatur ;") and that it does not matter whether the life be taken away when born or parturition prevented, for it is man that is to be, for the fruit is in the seed. In case of wilful abortion after the fortieth day, when the male was supposed to become animate, the embryo, in the tribunal of conscience, was *supposed to be a male.* Navarus attests this to be the practice.

Hippocrates is said to have taught a damsel how to get rid of a conception. This indeed is contrary to the oath taken by him, and to the high moral feeling of the man. The "oath" specially prohibits the procuring abortion. Several authors, however, hand down the reputed circumstance,

* *Apologeticus,* c. 9.

and, amongst others, that learned and conscientious Italian physician, Zacchia, in his great work, the *Questiones Medico-Legales*,* where he speaks of the errors of physicians punishable by law. In alluding to cases where physicians prescribe medicines to procure abortion, all know, he says, how great is the sin they commit; and he mentions, believing it as a fact, this case as given in Hippocrates, of whom he speaks with great regard, calling him, "*Noster Vir*"; and whom, quaintly enough he pronounces, very pious, *though a heretic*, (" *de Ethnico*"). Yet, he says, Hippocrates did not restrain himself from this crime, but procured abortion in a certain wench, giving the fact from the author himself (*Lib. de Nat. puer.* Num. iv.)

It is necessary to mention that the authenticity of the part of the works of Hippocrates, in which this passage occurs, is more than doubtful.

Zacchia also alludes to the fact that the ancient philosophers did not look upon abortion as a crime of such moment; as Aristotle pronounced it lawful, in order to diminish the number of children, to procure abortion before the fœtus arrived at feeling and life. He adds that "at present" the crime is forbidden both by human and divine laws; as he is rightly considered a homicide who procures

* Lib. vi, Q. vii, p. 889.

L

abortion of the animated fœtus. He then alludes to a fact that females seeking abortion should know, that during the means they may employ their own lives are in as great jeopardy as that of the fœtus they try to get rid of ; and he further says that those who try to bring on abortion are rightly punished by the laws, but that it is a question among jurists whether the same punishment should be meted to those who kill the animate as to those who destroy the inanimate fœtus. The more general opinion, he considers to be, that he who destroys the inanimate conception ought to be visited with extraordinary chastisement, but that he who destroys the animate should suffer the most public punishment.

Some writers laid it down that the fœtus becomes animate in three days; others, like Mercuralis, following some older writers, considered that the fœtus was perfected in seven days and endowed with life. Zacchia concludes that, although there is not the same end of the formation and increase of all (as in *Galen de Fœt. format.* cap. 1), yet it is better to adhere to Hippocrates ; and in order to strike a mean between conflicting authorities and opinions, he wishes to have it accepted that after the sixtieth day a female as well as a male be considered animate, and that he is guilty of homicide who procures to be cast out by abortion a more advanced conception of two months.

In 1532, the Emperor Charles V introduced the distinction of a vital and non-vital fœtus, instead of that which was previously known as an animate and inanimate one, as he considered this of a more obvious and easy decision, and not depending on any system, "either of creation, tradition, or infusion."

These opinions of philosophers and physiologists, as Dr. Beck truly remarks, while they influenced the laws, which in fact were based upon such opinions, on the subject of abortion, tended to encourage the practice; for, of course, as far as future accountability was concerned, there could be no sin in ejecting from the womb, a substance, in their opinion, wholly devoid of life; and, in any case where disgrace must be the consequence to the female and her family, as the result of illicit indulgence, recourse was almost sure to be had to a means so effectual, if successful, in screening their dishonour. As long as the embryo was considered merely "pars viscerum matris,"* the doctrine of the stoics, and also according to the law of Scotland, in what could be the crime? Subsequently to the philosophic teachings their doctrines

---

* Plutarch's *Morals*, vol. iii, p. 230.

were admitted, and different degrees of punishment were meted out according to the period of pregnancy when abortion was caused; or, in other words, according as the fœtus was animate or inanimate.*

Few things, probably, could show more clearly the ill effects, and at the same time prove the existence, of that "blind submission to authority," which Bacon so much bewails as restraining the progress of the human mind, than the long adhesion to those dicta of the philosophers. For here, without the slightest proofs on which to found accurate deductions, or even reasonable conjectures, it is gravely announced at what period life and soul join the previously inert mass; this period being considered by some sooner or later, according to the strength and warmth of the embryo, as if soul were to be forced, like mushrooms, according to the condition of mere matter. And still more absurd is the distinction between the period of animation of the male and that of the female—40 days for the one and 80 for the other. Can any thing be more pitiful than the dogmatism with which this doctrine was pronounced, or melancholy than the tenacity with which it was handed down even in the Christian period. See how trammelled

---

* Fodère, vol. iv, p. 382.

by this blind submission are the minds of the learned as well as pious ; as in the case of Zacchia, when he strives to strike a mean between jarring opinions, and to make 60 days the period at which animation occurs in both sexes !

But the distinction is wholly untenable. Life, there can be no doubt, is concomitant with conception. The germ that contains and shows in after age the very peculiarities of conformation of one or both parents, is endowed with the living principle from the first. The fiat has already gone forth, the soul has an existence, and he who destroys the embryo of a month puts out a life as effectually as he who destroys one of four or five. The old doctrine on this head is therefore justly exploded amongst modern physiologists. Everything tends to prove that life exists from the first moment of conception. In cases where the *death* of the embryo takes place it is generally soon expelled, and at all events soon begins to show signs of putrefaction, being then reduced indeed to the state of inert matter : which signs never appear while *life* exists.

This leads us to speak again of " quickening," and the doctrine obtaining until lately upon this head. This most fallacious of all fallacies on which to found a statute, as in the case of the law of

England, which both fixed the period of the commencement of life, thus agreeing with the old philosophers—at least as far as punishment for criminal abortion was concerned—and meted out its judgment accordingly; for Blackstone gravely lays it down that life is not considered to commence "before the infant is able to stir in the mother's womb." Granting for a moment that this was a fact, which it is not, see how worthless it is as a definition as regards *life in reality.* Who, for instance, can say when the infant first stirs? Certainly not the mother; for the child may stir often and often without the mother being conscious of it. The uterus is not so susceptible of impressions as to cause the first stir of the infant to be instantly conveyed to the maternal sensorium. Or, again, if the mother should be conscious of the very first movement of the child, it does not follow that *at the moment life is imparted* the infant must give intimation by stirring. On the contrary, the child may remain long quiescent after the acquisition, in a legal sense, of life. Further; one woman, endowed with high nervous susceptibility, may feel the motions of the fœtus at an early period of pregnancy; while another woman, of more obtuse sensibility, may not perceive the motions, if made, until a comparatively late period. Indeed some, having once and again felt, or supposed they felt, motion, may remain weeks upon weeks without experiencing a repetition of it, so much so that they often conclude, in consequence, that the child is dead.

Thus, then, the doctrine of the English law, so long applied, was equal both in dogmatism and absurdity to the dictum of the old philosophy; for assuredly he who procures abortion an hour *after quickening*, or, in other words, after the mother has felt the motions of the child, would be morally, *though not legally*, equally guilty of taking away life, if he should have procured abortion an hour before such motion was felt. Besides, such *fact* of quickening was left to the decision of the mother, who, if she swore she did not feel the child stir within her, might screen the person who had procured the abortion. So then, to procure abortion *before* "quickening," was punishable as felony, and by transportation; whereas *after* quickening, it was punishable by death! Yet life was equally destroyed in both cases.

It is fortunate for society, and at the same time cannot be too generally proclaimed, that the unworthy woman who endeavours to get rid of the child which she carries, by criminal expulsion from her womb, thus adding the deliberate sin of murder

to her former one of the passions ; the consequences
of which now make her look with anguish upon
the verdict which society may pass upon her if her
state should be found out, can succeed in her de-
signs only at the risk of her own life.  The attempt to procure abortion is bad enough on the
part of unmarried women, on whose state society
ought to look with some degree of compassion,
rather than drive them, by the cruel fiat that leaves
them as outcasts once their shame is known, to
commit a crime so heinous as that of infanticide.
But what can be said of married women who procure abortion sooner than have more children?
The strong, sometimes insurmountable, impulse
which shame gives to the feelings is here wanted,
and such people go about their deed of wickedness
in the most cold-blooded manner.  Medical prac-
titioners can testify to applications for the purpose
of procuring abortion by married women who do
not wish to have more children, and who appear to
think such a proceeding of little moment ; conscious, apparently, neither of the sinfulness of the
crime, if perpetrated, nor of the insult they offer
to a member of the medical profession by the mere
mention of such a proposition.  Cases are known
where retribution quickly followed these unhal-
lowed efforts ; and where women, previously in

robust condition, never more enjoyed health ; the entire system being visited by a host of ills previously unknown,—heart and stomach diseases, with their attendant dropsies, leaving frames weak and flabby, whose strength and tonicity were previously unimpaired. Often would some of these women in after life, when perhaps the child or children they had were carried away by the hand of death, give worlds for the further offspring of marriage, which the previous abuse of their own system rendered utterly hopeless.

At Stroud, 1860, a man named Hind, who pretended, falsely, to be in the medical profession, was sentenced to six years penal servitude for having used an instrument to procure abortion. The death of the poor girl ensued. She was advised to go to Hind. He used an instrument on Monday, and the child was born on Wednesday. She left on the Friday, though the prisoner wished her to remain till the Monday. She soon fell ill; and told the surgeon who attended her that, from what she could see, the child was a good sized one, and that Hind kept it. The girl added, *that ladies used to go to the prisoner in their carriages*, and that he got his bread by this kind of practice. The above account is from the *Medical Times and Gazette*, which adds, that "it is only too much to be feared that the number of those who carry on this sort of trade is greater than is generally supposed."

At Leicester, 1861, Mrs. Goddard undertook, for one guinea, to procure abortion on a woman, *the mother of nine children.* She saw the woman alone at her own house. On the woman's return home she was "taken ill, and died in a short period. From her statements, just before death, to her husband, who visited her, and from the appearances presented on *post-mortem* examination, no doubt could be felt that her death had been occasioned by the misconduct of the woman Goddard." The jury found a verdict of wilful murder against her. She was afterwards sentenced to death.

At Winchester Assizes, 1861, a man named Hooker, and two female accomplices, were convicted of having procured abortion in a young *married* woman. His charge was 20s., half down, the remainder when he succeeded. He used instruments; and said he had been sixteen years at that sort of business. He was sentenced to penal servitude for seven years; the two women, to six months imprisonment each. At Leicester, a similar case was brought forward, on a married woman also. A verdict of wilful murder was returned.

It appeared some time since that in Birmingham

there was a house where a system of producing abortion was regularly carried on. Something of the same kind appeared in Dudley. In this latter place (1860), " several young women residing there, named Newell, Wheeler, Hunt, and Bond, daughters of respectable parents, finding themselves in a pregnant condition, combined together to procure the means of abortion,—a step which has been, it is said, attended with nearly fatal consequences to themselves. The disclosures made by Sarah Hunt are said to have been of a most shocking description ; and she herself, it is feared, is almost beyond recovery. She is only seventeen years old, and like the others, previously bore a good character. She miscarried ; and the same result is anticipated in the case of the others. Two surgeons are in attendance. There are many disgusting details in connexion with this extraordinary affair, which do not admit of publication. The disclosures already made have produced a deep sensation in Sedgley and its neighbourhood." (*Med. Times and Gazette,* 1860.)

In the Birmingham business, a young woman died in the General Hospital, to whom a druggist, named White, had administered drugs in order to procure abortion. White also used instruments in a darkened room. Miscarriage ensued. She lost the use of her right arm and legs, and told a friend she did not think she should get well. In this case, the girl was sent to the house of a Mrs. Fisher until she got out of her trouble, without any person knowing it. Fisher was allowed 10s. a week by Frederick Bower. Neither Fisher nor her husband would consent to write to her friends until she made a vow that she would not divulge a word of what had been done to her to any one that came to see her. A verdict of wilful murder was brought in against White; and also against Mrs. Fisher, as an accessory before the fact.

How is it that women are not fully impressed with the sin of causing abortion? They certainly do appear unconscious of the magnitude of the crime; and this surely is strange and lamentable in the midst of well-paid religious teachers. The clergyman who ceases to battle with the tendency to this crime, as well as with that towards infanticide, in my opinion sadly neglects his duty. There is here a more fitting arena to do good, by those who really desire to do good, than can be found in many other places; and clerical exertions cannot here fail to meet a just reward.

The female not only risks her life in these attempts, but it often happens that, while her object is not gained, her own death ensues. Velpeau gives a case of the kind, where a woman produced violent abdominal inflammation by taking drops to procure abortion. She died on the eighth day, but no symptoms of abortion occurred. The child, in some of these attempts, has been known to be born alive, and to survive, even while the mother died from the effects of the medicine taken. A case of this kind is handed down by Fodère.*

In 1791, a cook, who was pregnant, took half an ounce of powdered cantharides, together with one ounce of sulphate of magnesia. She was seized with violent pains some hours afterwards, and was delivered of a living child. She suffered the greatest agony, and died on the following night. Numerous authorities establish the truth of the opinion given; not only that noxious drugs, taken with this intention, are always dangerous to the mother, but that they kill the mother frequently without affecting in the smallest degree the contents of the uterus. The feelings, to use no stronger expression, of a woman dying under such circumstances are not to be envied; and much less enviable still must be the feelings of any guilty partner of the crime, in witnessing, as may too often be done in such cases, the death alike of the

* Vol. iv, p. 436.

mother and fœtus. "Every woman who attempts to promote abortion, does it at the hazard of her life," says Bartley.* "There is no drug," says Dr. Male,† "which will produce miscarriage in women who are not predisposed to it, without acting violently on their system, and probably endangering their lives." Dr. G. Smith‡ says, "it has frequently happened that the unfortunate mother herself has been the sacrifice, while the object intended has not been accomplished." And Dr. Michael Ryan§ asserts, "there is no medicine which always procures abortion, and nothing but abortion; that there is none that does not endanger the lives of the mother and infant." Paris and Fonblanque‖ say "that medicines internally administered seldom procure abortion." They admit that violent medicines, by involving the uterus in the general shock, may bring on abortion, provided there exist a predisposition on the part of the woman. Burns¶ also adds his opinion as to strong cathartics inflaming the stomach and bowels; he thinks that when these medicines do produce abortion, the woman seldom survives.

* *Treatise on Forensic Medicine*, p. 5.
† *Epitome of Juridical Medicine.*
‡ *Forensic Medicine*, p. 295.   § *Med. Jurisprudence*, p. 270.
‖ Vol. iii, p. 90.    ¶ *Principles of Midwifery*, p. 283.

Rue is one of the things that have long had a good or evil report as regards their power of procuring abortion. It is mentioned by Hippocrates, Dioscorides, Pliny, and others of the older authors. Its use is attended with much danger to the mother. Helie* gives three cases of poisoning by it, where it was taken for the purpose of procuring abortion. The symptoms were " epigastric pain, violent and continued vomiting, inflammation and swelling of the tongue, salivation, colic, fever, thirst, disorder of the muscular system, manifested by tottering gait and irregular and convulsive movements of the body and limbs." Savin had an equal popularity, and an equal fatality attended its use. A case is mentioned by Mohrenheim where an infusion of savin was swallowed by a woman, thirty years of age, in order to cause abortion. Violent and incessant vomiting ensued. Some days elapsed, when she was seized with excruciating pains, followed by abortion, "fearful hæmorrhage from the uterus, and death." Fodère gives a case where a woman, in order to abort, took every morning one hundred drops of oil of savin during twenty days, and yet brought forth a living child. Dr. Christison† gives a case of Mr. Cookson, where a girl took a strong infusion

---

* Pereira, vol. i, p. 210.     † *Treatise on Poisons*, p. 531.

of savin leaves in order to procure abortion. Strangury, accompanied by violent pains, ensued, and in two days she miscarried, and died herself. Dr. Beck mentions a case recorded by Murray, where savin caused abortion, and at the same time killed the mother. The coroner's return for 1837-8 gives four cases where savin was administered in order to procure abortion. The mothers *died undelivered in three of these;* in the fourth, the child was killed.

These two drugs are given as instances of the effects of medicines popularly employed to a bad end. The same account might be given of most of those things which have been from time to time made use of; but the present is not a fitting occasion, and enough has been said to show how greatly those err who call such things into requisition.

That there are persons who obtain a living by the practice of causing abortion is well known, though not, it is to be hoped, to the extent that Devergie asserted of English midwifes. No amount of punishment should be considered too severe for wretches who disgrace humanity by the enormity of such offences. A patient of mine assures me that by using a certain medicine she can produce abortion in a few days. She also assures me of the fact that men are well known who for £5 will ensure abortion, and that she herself took a journey from London to Manchester to consult one of them. On her return she commenced taking his medicine, and I can answer for the *result*, as I was called in one night while she was suffering excruciating agony. From the symptoms I suspected she was about to abort, and made a vaginal examination. The bearing-down pains were very severe, and the uterus was evidently impregnated. From some remarks I made, she considered, as she afterwards told me, " that I knew too much for her," and suspected the state of affairs, and in consequence told the servant she should not again call in my services. She suffered much during the night, but the next morning I received word that I need not attend as she felt quite well. In fact she aborted during the night. She has the most perfect confidence that the "Doctor" she went to can at any time cause her to abort if pregnant, of which fact he himself assured her. She considered she might have had relief from my prescription, while she concealed the cause of her sufferings.

The difficulty which sometimes exists in procuring abortion is well shown by Professor Wägner* of Berlin. It was the case of " a young woman seven

---

* *London Medical Quarterly Review*, vol. ii, p. 487.

M

months gone with child, who had employed savin and other drugs with a view to produce a miscarriage. As these had not the desired effect, a strong leather strap was tightly bound round her body. This, too, availing nothing, her paramour (according to his own confession), knelt upon her, and compressed the abdomen with all his strength, without effecting the desired object. The man now trampled on the girl's person while she lay on her back; and as this also failed, he took a sharp-pointed pair of scissors, and proceeded to perforate the uterus through the vagina. Much pain and hæmorrhage ensued, but did not last long. The woman's health did not suffer in the least, and pretty much about the regular time a living child was brought into the world without any marks of external injury upon it. It died, indeed, four days afterwards, but its death could not be traced to the violence inflicted on the mother's person. All the internal organs appeared normal and healthy."

Velpeau* has shown the dangers attending attempts with instruments. He says, "Those who make use of them most frequently fail in obtaining their object, and succeed only in seriously injuring the womb. I once prescribed for a female in

---

* Meigs's *Velpeau*, p. 238, as quoted by Dr. Beck.

whom such attempts had brought on a flooding which conducted her to the verge of the grave; she suffered horribly from pain in the interior of the pelvis for two months, notwithstanding which abortion did not take place, and she is now a prey to a large ulcer on the neck of the womb. I opened the body of an unhappy creature who suffered from like attempts, which did not succeed any better than the one above mentioned."

M. Girard of Lyons mentions a similar instance. "In October 1828, a young woman, who became pregnant against her wishes, succeeded by such manœuvres only in producing an organic lesion of the uterus, which, after frightful sufferings, led her to the commission of suicide."

In the case mentioned by Wägner, the leather band used was the thong of a skate, and such a mode of procuring abortion has long been known. Hippocrates, in his *Aphorisms*, alludes to the fact, as does Galen in his *Commentaries;* the child being considered to be destroyed for want of nourishment.

A man was executed in 1811, at Stafford, for the murder of his wife. She was pregnant and he tried to bring on abortion by very violent means, elbowing her in bed, and rolling over her, etc. He succeeded not only in procuring abortion, but in killing his wife.* Dr. Campbell gives another case, where a woman was struck on the abdomen in the last month of her pregnancy by her husband. This caused an extensive detachment of the placenta and death of the fœtus. The woman herself died 51 hours afterwards. Madame La Chapelle mentions the case of a young woman who was pregnant, and having a very narrow pelvis, she hoped to bring on abortion by throwing herself from a height. Abortion did not ensue, but she herself died.

Where instruments have been used by the ignorant the woman fares little better than in the case of noxious drugs. The injury produced is so great that the female as often dies as the fœtus is destroyed. Inflammation of different kinds follows, of the pelvic viscera, the womb, or peritoneum; or injury of one form or another takes place so that the woman generally falls a sacrifice. The neck and body of the uterus are often pierced and irretrievably injured. Wooden skewers have been thrust into the body of the uterus, as appeared on a trial in the north of England some time since, where inflammation and mortification took place, and the woman died.† The prisoner was found guilty and executed.

---

* Dr. Smith's *Principles of Forensic Medicine*, p. 301.
† Taylor's *Medical Jurisprudence*, p. 284.

At the Leicester March Assizes, 1855, Charles Asher was tried for endeavouring to procure abortion on a married woman named Elizabeth Fletcher, whose husband was in America, where she was about to join him, but being pregnant took this method of preventing its being known. She died from the internal injuries inflicted by the prisoner, who was transported for 14 years.

This was a dreadful case, and goes far to show that the practice of criminal abortion is carried to a very great extent. Asher promised her that for two sovereigns he would cause her to abort. The woman told another person she was not going to *take* anything—taking would be of no use. She went three times to Asher, but he did not succeed, and the woman said, when her neighbours tried to dissuade her from going to him again, that, "*she would not pay all that money for nothing, and* THAT IF HE *could not do it there was a man at Nottingham who charged five pounds and she should go to him.* On Wednesday, February 7, he performed some operation on her, from which time she began to suffer pain. On Friday she was taken seriously ill, and on Saturday she was worse. Asher was sent for, and trembled very much when informed of her state. He said it *was the first case that had ever failed!* On the Tuesday following she died.

There were marks of contusions below the umbilicus on either side of the symphisis pubis. The muscles of the abdomen were infiltrated with pus and coagulated blood was found between them. The bladder was almost black and in a state of gangrene, having a large lacerated opening in its posterior part, and an aperture of considerable size in the corresponding part of the anterior wall of the uterus, two-thirds of the neck of which was detached from the body. The fœtus escaped into the bladder!

In East's *Pleas of the Crown,* mention is made of the case of Margaret Tinkler, tried at the Durham Assizes, 1781, for the murder of Janet Parkinson, by inserting pieces of wood into her womb. The deceased took to her bed on the 2nd of July, and died on the 23rd, being five months with child. The prisoner was a midwife. The delivery took place on the 10th of July; three days before which time the prisoner took her round the waist, and shook her violently five or six times, tossing her up and down. The child was born alive, but died instantly. Two holes were found in the womb; one mortified, the other much inflamed. There were other injuries.

Dr. Beck mentions another case, on the authority of Judge Hutchinson, of Vermont. Norman Cleveland was tried for the murder of Hannah Rose. She was pregnant by him; and he tried various means in vain in order to procure abortion. He then introduced a sharp-pointed instrument into the vagina, the woman almost instantly dying. There were six punctures in the neck of the uterus, in width from half to three-quarters of an inch each, as if made with a two-edged instrument. The iliac vein was wounded, and the abdomen filled with coagulated blood. He was sentenced to be hung; but this was afterwards commuted to five years hard labour in prison.

To show with what danger to the life of the female any attempt to introduce instruments into the uterus by inexperienced persons, is attended, it is only necessary to describe the case which terminated fatally even in the hands of so good an anatomist as Dr. W. Hunter, who attempted to introduce an instrument for the purpose of rupturing the membranes, in the case of a young woman, at about the third month of pregnancy. "He found that he several times punctured the cervix uteri, and the case terminated fatally." "If this happened," says Dr. Robert Gooch, " to one of so much anatomical knowledge and skill, how much more probable must it be in the hands of those ignorant men, by whom, for the purpose alluded to, the operation is sometimes undertaken! No doubt these attempts often prove fatal; but the murdered do not tell tales."

Many other cases could be mentioned; but enough have now been brought forward to show the certain risk women run who employ such unnatural means.

So much depends upon the medical man in these cases, both as to the immediate acquittal or punishment of the female, as well as to her future reputation, that it behoves him well and carefully to weigh all the circumstances of the case; that while he may not attempt to screen the guilty, he will not, at the same time, allow any suspicious looking circumstances, and which may be purely accidental, to influence him in a way that might tend to the prejudice of the innocent. Circumstances are often met with where the life or death of the female, or what is often more, the honour and happiness of an innocent woman is placed in his hands. He should be chary in giving opinions on the many questions that will be put to him by officious bystanders.

We cannot be too grateful that, as a body, the

medical profession has kept itself high above all temptations to meddle with this unclean thing. The strict moral feeling they have ever shown in this respect is greatly to their credit; and however much they may be scandalized by individual instances of criminality and unworthiness in this, as in other things; still the self-respect, probity, and dignity evidenced by the entire body is fully acknowledged. The most poorly requited of the professions, it is peculiarly laid open to temptations of irregularity; and especially in cases of quackery these temptations have been doubled by the open-mouthed gullibility of a people who will be cheated. Quackery in all times has existed, and has flourished as in England, where the people are willing dupes. But in all cases has the profession kept aloof, and even warned the deluded people of the risk they ran;—and indeed great has been the risk up to this last, and most impudent, and most untenable imposture—the homœopathic delusion.

Had that delusion anything in it, the lie would be given to all previous history, and to all previous efforts of the human mind. The labours of ages must go for nothing; and the experience handed down from generation to generation, to be improved upon as time goes on, is utterly worthless. All philosophical theories of progress must be thrown to the winds; and Bacon, with the inductive sciences, must be ignored as worse than useless; for they only lure us to the loss of time which might be better employed. For is not here Hahnemann and his disciples, who have absolutely sprung to perfection, without trouble and without study; in an art that has taken century after century of hardworking, highminded, and honourable men, in an endeavour to bring—and unsuccessfully to bring, up to the present—to something like perfection.

But there is no danger for the divine art of healing; and this last quackery, which promised to be so gigantic an error, has already collapsed. Having nothing of vitality in it—being simply the "baseless fabric of a vision"—its impending dissolution will leave no wreck behind. Belying their professions by their acts, the disciples of this new creed,—if creed it can be called,—have long been known, in cases of real disease and where great danger threatened, to pitch their globules to the winds, and to fly to those good old "allopathic" remedies which stood the test of time. No blame could attach to them for this, had they not done it furtively; still pretending their unshaken faith in infinitesimal doses. Some, indeed, as in America,—and much to their honour and credit be it spoken,—having found out the absolute hollowness of homœopathy, publicly acknowledged their errors, and freed themselves from the cheat.    Thoughtless heads and idle hands in high places did much to draw men from their allegiance to legitimate medicine ; but it is to be hoped, that error being detected, reparation will be made to an outraged profession !

In this business also, of abortion, have we to lament that any member, however lowly, should have so far forgotten what is due to his profession and to society, not to mention higher motives, as to outrage the one and do a wicked injustice to the other.    This sad transaction will serve to point a moral, and may have its good effects if it only further tends to show, what I have endeavoured throughout to prove, that the woman who seeks to procure abortion by criminal means can only do so at the risk of her own life.

In October 1861 an inquest was held on the body of Eliza Garrett, of Limehouse Fields, aged 34, who, it was alleged, died from injuries caused by a medical man named Vale.    The husband of the woman was an accomplice in the crime, and was afterwards committed to prison for wilful murder.    This husband before the magistrate denied that he desired his wife to procure abortion, but said he knew she was in the habit of going to the prisoner Vale; and that she told him Vale had used instruments on her in order to procure abortion, and had given her medicine.

Lucy Reynolds deposed that she was called to see the deceased, who was suffering great pain. This woman was a next-door neighbour, but did not know she was ill before the time she was sent for. On being asked what was the matter with her, she said she did not know, but on further pressing admitted it was a miscarriage. The wife of the prisoner Vale had by this time arrived, and one child was born, and shortly after, another— both dead. Vale himself was then present, and shortly after went away. The woman had been very ill during the night, and next morning expressed a fear that she should not recover. On being pressed to tell the truth, she charged witness not to tell anybody, and then acknowledged that she had been to Mr. Vale, and that her husband had persuaded her to go. She said that Vale had used an instrument with teeth in it, and opening with a spring in the end, and that he was to have half-a-guinea for his services. He had used the instrument on two occasions. Vale called the Saturday before the poor woman died, and she was then delirious. On a *post-mortem* examination three indistinct marks were found upon the mouth of the womb, which the medical witness thought might have been the result of puncture by the instrument referred to, and the exciting cause of inflammation. A verdict of wilful murder was returned against Vale, and the grand jury afterwards returned a true bill for manslaughter against him.

Shortly after this, Mrs. Vale, whose practices, in conjunction with her husband, were reported to be of a most questionable character, was charged at the Thames Police Court with the serious offence of "administering to Ann Horne a noxious drug, with intent to procure abortion." Mrs. Vale administered medicine, after which Horne retched violently. A second dose was given, and the woman complained of great suffering, "as if all her inside were coming from her at once." *They expected a miscarriage* from what Mrs. Vale said. A witness, Parkins, a married woman, who was by during the time, said, *she did not think it was very wrong to procure a miscarriage —that she did not know it was wrong to do it!* Abortion ensued, and evidence was given as to the fearful condition of the patient.

The following most creditable resolutions have

been lately unanimously adopted by the Scott County Medical Society (Iowa), United States of America.

"Whereas, the medical profession are everywhere cognisant of the fact that the crime of criminal abortion is fearfully prevalent, and increasing in all classes of society; and whereas, the progress of civilisation and the spread of religion appear not to have had the effect of diminishing this species of iniquity; therefore be it resolved,—

"1. That the members of this society will cooperate with the American Medical Association, and other organisations of the kind, in using every effort to disseminate a knowledge of the criminal nature of practices which are too often regarded as harmless, and frequently resorted to by many who would shudder at the thought of destroying the life of a human being.

"2. That the members of this society unite in sentiment with the opinion of the best and most learned men of the profession in all parts of the world, that the foetus is a living being from the earliest period of gestation, the wilful destruction of which, except when required for the preservation of the life of the mother, is a crime as monstrous as infanticide, and its perpetrators should be regarded as felons by the laws of man, as they must be by every precept of morality.

"3. That every member of this society, who may be known to yield to the solicitation of any party for the purposes above indicated, shall forfeit his membership, and be regarded as unworthy of fellowship by all honourable physicians.

"4. That it shall be considered the duty of every physician, when application for such purpose is made, not only to decline promptly, but to exert his personal influence to the utmost to prevent its accomplishment, by explaining its criminal character, and removing as far as possible the erroneous opinions which are so generally prevalent regarding the life of the foetus.

"5. That we denounce the common practice of newspaper proprietors in publishing advertisements which are calculated to encourage the practice of criminal abortion, as one prolific cause of a vast amount of crime and immorality, for which such newspaper editors and proprietors are thereby in a great degree responsible.

"6. That we likewise denounce the practice of many druggists in keeping for sale and dispensing such preparations as are known to be used for the purpose of procuring abortion, which practice is no less reprehensible than to furnish poison when knowingly purchased with murderous intent, and by which all such druggists are *participes criminis* in the evil work of corrupting good morals, and wilfully engaged in aiding and assisting in the perpetration of a crime which should be held in abhorrence by every member of a civilised and Christian community."

# III.

## HISTORY OF INFANTICIDE AS IT PREVAILED IN DIFFERENT COUNTRIES AND AGES.

FROM the period when the "voice of the blood of Abel" arose from the ground unto heaven, the Almighty was ever provoked by, and heavily punished, the crime of murder; and that first murder following so quickly on the sin of disobedience, which had cost the transgressors, and has cost the whole human race so much, although not punished by death, was visited by the most severe afflictions, the perpetrator of it being pronounced "accursed," and being driven forth "a fugitive and a vagabond upon the earth."[*]

Whatever might have been the punishment of murder before the flood, we know from Moses what it was after that period, viz., death to the murderer:—" Whosoever shall shed man's blood, his

---

[*] Genesis c. iv.

blood shall be shed: for man was made to the image of God."*

In the laws given to Moses, the Almighty evinces the greatest abhorrence of murder and murderers, expressly and most strongly forbidding the former, and appointing avengers of such deeds; and in no cases have His denunciations been stronger than in those where children, offered up in sacrifice, were the subjects.

Murder could only be expiated by the death of the murderer. One man might lawfully kill another, only, 1st. When a murderer was found by the avenger of blood out of his place of refuge; 2ndly. In self-defence; 3rdly. In defence of another Israelite.†

That human sacrifices were ever offered seems a melancholy contemplation, as a consequence of our fallen nature; but it is no less true than melancholy that such have been offered: and if the contemplation be more painful and repulsive in one series of cases than in another it is in the cases of children— in the massacre, truly, *of the Innocents.* Infanticide,‡ indeed, from whatever motive, presents mur-

---

* Genesis ix, 6.

+ *Ancient History of the Jews,* p. 127.

‡ The poet of Chalcis, Lycophron, is the authority for the Grecian deity being called *Infanticida,* which was thought to have been applied to Hecate or Diana, in one of her other forms.

der in one of its most revolting forms, whether perpetrated wholesale, as in the pagan nations of antiquity ; and even amongst the "chosen people" when they forgot the Lord ; a burnt offering to the "idols of Canaan ;" a passing "through the fire to Molech ;" or amongst some modern nations and peoples who know not "*The Word ;*" or finally as occurring in isolated cases amongst Christian people.

The Christian stands amazed and confounded that such things should be in any state, and humbled by sorrow and by a feeling of abasement when he considers that the blood of children "crieth from the earth" to God, even in our own days.

We know that before and after the deluge the heathen gods or demons had human beings sacrificed to them, and especially of the children of those sacrificing: and we learn from many ancient authors that in Phœnicia and in ancient Egypt such sacrifices were common. This is said by Sanchoniatho, Manetho, Pausanias, Diodorus Siculus, Philo, Plutarch, and Porphyry, and that such took place long even before Abraham's time. Sanchoniatho, in speaking of the mystical sacrifice of the Egyptians, says, "It was the custom among the ancients, in times of great calamity, in order to prevent the ruin of all, for the rulers of a city or nation to sacrifice to the avenging deities the most beloved of their children as the price of redemption. They who were devoted for this purpose were offered mystically; for *Cronus*, whom the Phœnicians call *Il*, and who, after his death was deified and instated in the planet which bears his name, when king, had by a nymph of the country called Anobret an only son, who on that account is styled *Jeoud*, for so the Phœnicians still call an only son; and when great danger from war beset the land, he adorned the altar, and invested his son with the emblems of royalty, and sacrificed him."*

Human sacrifices were not offered in Egypt in the time of Herodotus, nor would he believe that they ever had been; for he says, "the fable as if Hercules was sacrificed to Jupiter in Egypt was feigned by the Greeks, who were entirely unacquainted with the nature of the Egyptians and their laws; for how could they sacrifice men, with whom it is unlawful to sacrifice any brute beast, boars and bulls, and pure calves and ganders only excepted."†

---

* Cory's *Ancient Fragments*, p. 16: London, 1832. Also, Sir John Marsham's *Chronicon*, p. 76-300. Cory's *Sanchoniatho* (Phœnix, New York, 1835).

† Cory's *Ancient Fragments*, p. 301.

Yet is there little doubt that such things were. "They relate that of old the (Egyptian) kings sacrificed such men as were of the same colour with *Typho* at the sepulchre of Osiris."* Typho, called also Seth or Baal, was the representation of the evil spirit.

"Manetho relates that they burnt Typhonean men alive in the city of Idythia (or Ilythia), and scattered their ashes like chaff that is winnowed; and this was done publicly and at appointed seasons in the dog days."†

"The barbarous nations did a long time admit of the slaughter of children, as of a holy practice, and acceptable to the gods; and this, both private persons, and kings, and entire nations, practise at proper seasons."

Whiston believes, from the proofs afforded by Sir John Marsham and Bishop Cumberland, that human sacrifices were frequent long before the days of Abraham, both in Phœnicia and Egypt; and that this continued in many places, though not in Egypt, to the third if not to the fifth century of Christianity.‡

Juvenal's account, that while the Egyptians found deity in an onion they ate human flesh, is a strange one.

---

* Diodorus Siculus, p. 78.     † Plutarch, p. 78.
‡ Whiston's Josephus, *Dissert.* 2.

" Porrum et cæpe nefas, aut frangere morsu.
  O sanctas gentes, quibus hæc nascuntur in hortis
  Numina!       \*        \*        \*
  Carnibus humanis vesci licet.
        \*        \*        \*        \*

  Labitur hic quidam, nimiâ formidine cursum
  Præcipitans, capiturque : ast illum in plurima sectum
  Frustra et particulas, ut multis mortuus unus
  Sufficiret, totum corrosis ossibus edit
  Victrix turba."                 *Juv. Sat.* xv.

"The Phœnicians, descendants of the Canaanites, when they were in great danger by war, by famine, or by pestilence, sacrificed to Saturn one of the dearest of their people, whom they chose by public suffrage for that purpose; and Sanchoniatho's history is full of such sacrifices."\*

"In Arabia, the Dumatii sacrificed a child every year."†

"The human sacrifices that were enjoined by the Dodonean oracle, mentioned in Pausanias' *Achaics*, in the tragical story of Coresus and Calirrhoe, sufficiently intimate that the Phœnician and Egyptian priests had set up this Dodonean oracle before the time of Amosis, who destroyed that barbarous practice in Egypt.‡

Human sacrifices were never offered to the Almighty by his command; and when he wished

---

\* Porphyry, p. 77.             † Ibidem.
‡ Cumberland's *Sanchoniatho,* p. 378.

to test the love and obedience towards him of Abraham, for whom he had done so much, and found the faithful patriarch ready to obey the awful command and to offer Isaac, he himself substituted a sufficient oblation instead of the testimony of honour which his servant was ready to grant.* The warning voice soon told him that it was not out of a desire for human blood that the command had been given, but to test his obedience; and the ram was then produced for the sacrifice. It is not necessary to enter into any speculations put forward whether Abraham had indulged in any hopes that God would not demand the sacrifice, or that if he did he would again raise Isaac from the dead, or at all events "multiply Abraham's seed exceedingly," according to the promise. Granted that hope, the last to depart, was strong in the breast of Abraham, it would be but a poor compliment to his faith and fidelity to suppose otherwise than that he went forth with unquestioning devotion to offer to the "giver of all good things" the sacrifice he demanded.

We do not find any punishment in the laws of Moses for the crime of infanticide, more than the general law of one of the commandments given to him for his people, "thou shalt not kill." From

---

* Josephus, lib. 1, cap. xiii.

this, and from the character of the Jews at the time, we may well infer that the crime was unknown. A crime so heinous could scarcely be perpetrated at such a period without a punishment being specially awarded for it, as the punishment for murder is particularly specified. Bearing on this subject we have—"If men quarrel with each other, and one strike a woman with child, and she miscarry indeed, but live herself, he shall be answerable for as much damage as the woman's husband shall require, and as arbiters shall award. But if her death shall ensue thereupon he shall render life for life."*

Here there was no "*animus*" as against the infant, and therefore no punishment awarded for its death; but provision could scarcely be made for a case of this kind without at the same time alluding to the atrocious crime of infanticide, if it existed. And as incentives to such a crime, perhaps the consequences of the dreadful sin of the daughters of Lot, the shame and sense of degradation with which it cannot have failed to be accompanied, must have been as strong as it was well possible it could have been, did such tendencies prevail. Moreover, purity of morals was essentially an element of the laws of Moses; while "the

---

* Exodus xxi, 22, 23.

heathen religions were systems of mere ceremonies, on the observance of which it was imagined that the prosperity of the several states depended." "The purest morality, the most favourable to private and public happiness was the principal object of the system" of Moses.[*]

Philo Judeus, the contemporary of Josephus, says, if the child were unfashioned, or not fully formed, a fine was inflicted. "But if the child which was conceived had assumed a distinct shape in all its parts, having received all its proper connective and distinctive qualities, he shall die; for such a creature as that is a man, whom he has slain while still in the workshop of nature." Vol. iii, p. 330 (Bohn).

While the *Messiah*, too, was expected amongst the Jews, and while this expectation was cherished with such devotion, it would seem impossible that this crime could have been even contemplated; and besides, barrenness was considered one of the greatest reproaches amongst Jewish women. When, again, the handmaid of Sarah perceived "that she was with child she despised her mistress." And Sarah said to Abram—"Thou dost unjustly with me: I gave my handmaid unto thy bosom, and she perceiving herself with child *despiseth me.*

---

[*] Priestly in *Universal History*, Art. *Moses.*

The Lord judge between me and thee." "Give me children," said Rachel to her husband Jacob, "or I shall die." And again, when she conceived and bore a son,—"God hath taken away my reproach." And of Anna, one of the wives of Eleana,—"Her rival also afflicted her and troubled her exceedingly, insomuch that she upbraided her that the Lord had shut up her womb."

Indeed, we find the Israelites often horrified at these sacrifices. When the King of Moab was overthrown, "he took his eldest son that should have reigned in his stead, and offered him for a burnt offering upon the wall; and there was great indignation in Israel, and presently they departed from him and returned to their own country."

The Almighty severely condemned the pagan nations for their idolatrous sacrifices of children, and warned the Jews against such proceedings :— "Thou shalt not give any of thy seed to be consecrated to the idol Moloch, nor defile the name of thy God." * * * "If any man of the children of Israel, or of the strangers that dwell in Israel, give of his seed to the idol Moloch—dying, let him die; the people of the land shall stone him."* "For they have done to their gods all the abominations which the Lord abhorreth, offering their

---

* Leviticus xviii, 21 ; xx, 2.

sons and daughters, and burning them with fire."
"Neither let there be found any one among you
that shall expiate his son and daughter, making
them pass through the fire."* *Beware lest you
imitate them*, after they are destroyed at thy
coming in, and lest thou seek after their ceremonies, saying, As these nations have worshipped
their gods, so will I also worship."†

So that to this period it does not require that a
punishment should be named for a crime that
most probably did not exist amongst the Jews;
indeed, verse 30, as above, would seem to settle
that point —*beware lest you imitate them;* and
so, chap. xviii, v. 10, "Neither let there be found
any one among you," etc.

But at a subsequent period, when the Jews held
intercourse with surrounding nations, we find that
they erred grievously in this respect, and that
severe punishments were meted out to them.
Thus of the "wicked reign of Achaz,"‡ "making
his son pass through fire according to the idols of
the nations which the Lord destroyed before the
children of Israel. It was he that burned incense
in the valley of Benennom and consecrated his
sons in the fire according to the manner of the

---

* Deuteronomy xii, 30; xviii, 10.        † Ibid. xii, 31.
‡ 4 Kings xvi, 3.

nations which the Lord slew at the coming of the children of Israel."*    And so of Manasses, chap. xxxiii, " And they sacrificed their sons and their daughters to devils."†   " *And they shed innocent blood*, the blood of their sons and of their daughters which they sacrificed to the idols of Canaan.‡ "—— to burn their sons and their daughters in the fire which I commanded not, nor thought I on in my heart. * * * and they have filled this place with the blood of innocents."§   " And thou hast taken thy sons and thy daughters whom thou hast borne to me ; and hast sacrificed the same to them to be devoured."   " And I polluted them in their own gifts, when they offered all that opened the womb, for their offences."||   " *And those merciless murderers of their own children. * * * And those parents sacrificing with their own hands helpless souls.*"¶

We find Queen Athalia murdering her grand-children in order to reign herself (IV Kings, xi, 1).   In the days of King Achab, Hiel built Jericho and sacrificed children (III Kings, c. xvi, v. 34).

King Josias abolished idolatry, and with a strong hand put a stop to those dreadful sacrifices ; " and

---

* 2 Chronicles xxviii, 3.   † Psalm cv, 37, 38.   ‡ Isaiah lvii, 5.
§ Jerem. vii, 3-5.   || Ezekiel xvi, xx.   ¶ Wisdom xii, 4, 6.

he defiled Topheth that no man should consecrate there his son or daughter through fire to Molech."

The Moabites sacrificed both in the open air and on mountains, and in temples in the city built to their idols. They offered human victims on extraordinary occasions, according to the Phœnician custom. Amongst the Ammonites, also, as in neighbouring nations, human victims were offered up to their idol or king, Moloch—one of the seven receptacles in his hollow image being opened for the offering of a child. The valley of the sons of Hinnom, near Jerusalem, was so called from the shrieks of children sacrificed; as also Tophet, signifying a drum, as used to drown the cries of those about to be sacrificed.

When Pharaoh, king of Egypt, found the Israelites getting stronger and more numerous than his own people, among other notable schemes of oppression he hit upon one likely enough to exterminate them if it could have been carried out. He commanded the midwives of the Hebrew women, when attending at the time of delivery,—"if it be a man child, kill it." Pharaoh charged all his subjects to cast into the river whatsoever should be born of the male sex; yet, by a signal providence, the great avenger of the wrongs and oppressions of his countrymen—named because he was taken out of that water in which the king of Egypt intended all his race should perish—the mighty law-giver of Israel, Moses, when placed "in a basket made of bulrushes," and "left in the sedges by the river's brink," was saved by Thermutis, the daughter of this same king—the destined instrument of many afflictions on those oppressors of his people, who, knowing their worth, would neither treat them justly nor let them go.

Josephus[*] distinctly says these midwives were Egyptians, and that by reason of their relation to the king, they would not be likely to disobey his orders; and that Pharaoh further commanded that if any parents should save their male children, they, with their females should be destroyed. This was a dreadful affliction to the Hebrews, who were thus not only deprived of their sons, but made subservient to the destruction of them, "and to their own gradual dissolution."

To such straits were the miserable inhabitants driven during the siege of Jerusalem by Titus Cæsar, that Mary, the daughter of Eleazar, eminent for her family and wealth, slew her child, roasted him, and having eaten one half, concealed the other. When the seditious part of the people, prowling about, got the scent of food, they threat-

---

[*] Josephus, lib. ii, chap. ix.

ened to kill her if she did not give them what food she had prepared. She then brought forth what was left of her son, and they stood horror-struck at the sight. Upon this the whole city was full of the horrid transaction, and without the walls some of the besiegers could hardly believe the tale; some pitied, and some became more embittered against the Jews, and Titus, in his anger, resolved on the extirpation of the nation,—"that the sun might never shoot his beams on a city where the mothers feed on the flesh of their children, and where the fathers drive them to such extremities."*

While Tacitus, with an extraordinary amount of prejudice, gives his account of the history, customs, and religion of the Jews, grossly misrepresenting them on many points, he says that no man is allowed to put his children to death;† and this evidence, from such a source, is of the more weight, as he was a well-known enemy to the race; and shortly before says that amongst themselves nothing is unlawful.‡ The strictness and severe penalties of the Jewish law sufficiently refute this calumny.

---

* Josephus, *Bella Judeorum*, lib. vi, cap. iii. Tacitus, *Hist.*, lib. v.

† "Nam et necare quemquam ex agnatis nefas," lib. v. c. v.

‡ "Inter se nihil est illicitum."

The Jews, however, had great power over their children ; as in the case of an unruly and disobedient son, they were to bring him before the ancients of the city, and laying their complaint before them, "The people of the city shall stone him and he shall die."*

At the siege of Samaria by the Syrians, the famine was so great that a woman ate her own child :—"And as the King of Israel was passing by the wall, a certain woman cried out to him, saying, Save me, my lord, O King,—And the King said to her : What aileth thee ? And she answered : This woman said to me : Give thy son, that we may eat him to-day, and we will eat my son to-morrow.

"So we boiled my son, and ate him. And I said to her on the next day, Give thy son that we may eat him. And she hath hid her son."

The dreadful "massacre of the innocents," in the time of the infamous Herod, when "he was troubled and all Jerusalem with him;" and already steeped to the lips in blood ; and hated as he and his family were by the whole nation, is too well known to require dwelling on. Herod, thinking of his earthly kingdom only, feared it was in danger from the *Saviour*, and when those he sent

---

* Deuteronomy xxi, 18, 21.

forth did not return to Jerusalem, he, perceiving that he was deluded by the wise men, was exceeding angry; and sending, killed all the men children that were in Bethelem, and in all the borders thereof, from two years old and under, according to the time when he had diligently inquired of the wise men."*

I am informed by a Jewish friend, that the detestable crime is almost unknown amongst the Jews of the present day. What a happy exemption!

In the progress of Xerxes from Doriscus through Greece, when he came to the bridge thrown across the river Strymon, and heard that a certain place on their road was called the "nine ways," the magi having previously offered up a sacrifice of white horses; nine youths and as many virgins of the natives were buried alive. Herodotus† says this custom of burying alive was common in Persia, and that he had been told Amestris, the wife of Xerxes, in advanced age caused fourteen children of illustrious birth to be buried alive in honour of the deity who existed, as they thought, under the earth. We may well believe such a deed of a woman who so cruelly mutilated her

---

* St. Matthew ii, 16.
† Herodotus, lib. vii (Polymnia), cap. cxiv.

O

own sister-in-law, the wife of Masistes,[*] cutting off her breasts and throwing them to the dogs; and afterwards her nose, ears, lips, and tongue, and sending her home in this condition, because the daughter of this unfortunate woman had an intrigue with the husband of Amestris, old Xerxes himself.

The Greeks sometimes quickly disposed of their children, either by putting them to death or leaving them exposed, in various places, to whatever might chance. The latter had the sanction of law, and was rather encouraged by law-givers. Sometimes the parents did not wish their children destroyed, in exposing them; but trusted to chance as to their being taken up by some one. To do this they called ἐκτίθεσθαι, as expressing a less severe intention; or, ἀποτίθεσθαι, when done with a desire to destroy, as when cast into ἀποθέται. Female infants were more especially exposed.[†]

The Thebans, to their eternal honour, held this crime in detestation, and made its committal, *a capital offence.* Exposure was also forbidden.[‡] Ælian says that the Thebans were the only exception, of all the states of Greece, to the practice of

---

[*] Herodotus, lib. ix, cap. cvii.
[†] Ibidem, lib. ix (Calliope), cap. cvii-cxii.
[‡] Aristot., *Polit.* vii, 16.

exposing children; and Schefferus, in his *Annotations*, also shows that this conduct of the Thebans was different to the law and practice of the other part of the Greeks — the Athenians more especially.* The father was obliged to present them to the magistrate, and give proof that he was unable to rear them. They might then be purchased by any one and placed as slaves.† The place for exposure in Athens was called *cynosarges*, one of the *gymnacia*.

The Lacedæmonians scourged their children, death occasionally resulting, in honour of Diana Orthia.

One of the laws of Lycurgus was that the Spartan virgins should be married without portions; because neither want should hinder a man, nor riches induce him, to marry contrary to his inclinations. This law was in many respects very meritorious, tending to the preservation of female equally as of male children; and very different to the absurd custom of the Hindoos, whose ideas of degradation from having female children, owing to the portion they were expected to give with them at marriage; tended so much to perpetuate amongst

---

* Elian. var. Hist. l. i, c. vii, " Contra morem legesque reliquorum Grecorum et imprimis Atheniensium."

† Barthelemy's *Travels of Anacharsis*, vol. iii, p. 185.

them the horrible system of infanticide. It is to
be regretted, however, that no matter how strong
the bands of natural affection might be, parents,
particularly among the Lacedæmonians, were not
even allowed to rear what children they pleased,
but were obliged to take them to a place called
Lesche,* where the most ancient men of their
court examined them. If the child were strong
and well-proportioned it was allowed to live and
be educated, a certain portion of land being given
to maintain it ; but if weakly and deformed it was
cast into a place called Apotheta, a deep cavern
near Mount Taygetus ; the judges concluding that,
as nature had not made it hale and strong, its life
could be of no advantage to itself or the public.
The propagation of children was looked upon as
the only end of marriage.†

It is worth remarking, in contradistinction to
the absolute power of the Roman parents, and to
that of the Grecian States generally, that at seven
years of age the Lacedæmonian boys were placed
in public schools, no Lacedæmonian being allowed
to educate his sons in any other form than that
permitted by law.

So anxious was Lycurgus to have a nation of

---

* Λέσχη.
† Langhorne's Plutarch, vol. i, p. 177-180, 254.

soldiers, by preserving every strong infant, that this wise man, who, according to Mitford,* "carried his views far beyond those of ordinary legislators," made it a matter of no consequence whom the father of the child might be, provided it was a fine one"; contrary to the general feeling throughout Greece as to the sanctity of marriage.

Even the "divine Plato," following the institutions of the Cretans and Spartans, took away from the sanctity of marriage by making it a temporary instead of a lasting contract, lest the offspring should be claimed as belonging to the father, instead of to the state ; and of course the state reared them, not from affection, but from the benefit, they, as healthy children, were likely to confer on itself. He also alludes to the practice of procuring abortion. In his *Philosophical Republic*, as alluded to by Malthus,† Plato directed the inferior citizens to be matched with inferior females ; and their offspring, unlike those of the better class, which were to be brought up, were, together with those who were imperfect in their limbs, to be buried in some unknown place. When persons went beyond the probable age of child-bearing they were allowed more latitude of inter-

---

* Mitford's *History of Greece*, vol. i, p. 115-117.
† Malthus, b. 1, c. xii.

course; but no child was to be brought to light, and should one by accident be born alive, it was to be exposed in the same manner as if the parents were not able to support it.

The Pelasgians in times of scarcity offered every tenth child as a sacrifice of propitiation.

It does not appear so clear, by the laws of Solon, whether children were exposed, but such may be inferred, both from the fact that the custom, with the good exception of the Thebans, was general in Greece; as well as that the practice was defended by Aristotle and spoken of as a common one.[*] According to those laws the parents had full right of pronouncing on the life or death of their children. When the father could not bring up his child or saw certain defects of conformation, he turned aside his eyes, and the child was instantly carried away to be exposed or put to death.[†]

Aristotle[‡] seems quite at home on the subject of abortion; and treats it as a very light and harmless affair provided the mother had not "quickened." Indeed, state reasons seem to have overcome all others with these philosophers, so that they held and commanded that children naturally

---

[*] *Univ. Hist.*, vol. i, p. 175 (Lond.).
[†] Barthelemy's *Travels of Anacharsis*, vol. ii, p. 418.
[‡] *Polit.*, vii, 21.

feeble should be exposed; or that the children of a family having reached a certain number, any future ones should be destroyed in the womb before life and sensation were imparted! And yet, had not men's minds been then unenlightened by the religion of love, and consequently swayed by a false philosophy, something might have been expected against the crime of *filicide*, from *that Solon*, who, when asked why "he had fixed no punishment for him who had killed his parents," replied, that such a thing had never been known or heard of, and that, therefore, to provide against such a crime, specially, would be the way to introduce it;* and the Roman lawgivers, who took such good care of themselves in their laws against parricide, might have allowed nature, with some chance of success, to plead to their stony hearts in favour of the helpless offspring of their own bodies. The Romans considered the parricide undeserving of the common light, and therefore placed a hood on him, sewed him up alive in a sack,† an ape, a dog, and a cock being his companions, and he was thus

---

* Sapiente fecisse dicitur, cùm de eo nihil sanxerit, quod antea commissum non erat; ne, non tam prohibere, quam admonere, videretur. *Cic.* Pro Rosc. Amer. (*n.* 70).

† 'Culcus,'—hence this mode of punishment, afterwards so called.

thrown into the sea, a lake, or river.*   They considered the river would have been polluted had they thrown him naked into it, nor would they allow him to be devoured by wild beasts lest the latter might be rendered still more ferocious.   He was thus left to die so that his bones never touched the earth :—" Ita vivunt, dum possunt, ut ducere animam de cælo non queant ; ita moriuntur, ut eorum ossa terra non tangant."†

To the inquiries of Herodotus concerning Troy he was told that Helen, not being found in the captured city, the Greeks went in pursuit of her into Egypt.   Menelaus, who went himself, was honourably entertained by the king, Proteus, and Helen was restored to him with all her treasures; but heedless of all this, he committed a great enormity against the Egyptians ; for adverse winds preventing his departure, he took two children of the people of the country, and with great barbarity offered them in sacrifice.‡   This kind of sacrifice was frequent in Greece, but detestable in Egypt.§ Exposure of children was not allowed in Egypt,

---

* The *Projectio in profluentem.*

+ *Cic.* Pro sexto Roscio Amerino *(note,* Murphy's Tacitus, *Manners of the Germans.)*

‡ Beloe's Herodotus, Jones's *Classical Library*, p. 108.

§ Larcher.

and Strabo praises the people on that account.* Virgil alludes to the sacrifice of Iphigenia, the daughter of Agamemnon:

> "Isque adytis hæc tristia dicta reportat;
> Sanguine placâstis ventos et virgine cæsâ.
> Cùm primùm Iliacas, Danai, venistis ad oras;
> Sanguine quærendi reditus, animâque litandum
> Argolicâ."    *    *    *
>
>              Virg. Æn. II, 115.

Also to that of Polyxena, the daughter of Priam—

> "O felix una ante alias Priameia virgo
> Hostilem ad tumulum Trojæ sub mœnibus altis
> Jussa mori."
>
>              Æn. III, 321.

Ovid refers to the sacrifice of Polyxena at the tomb of Achilles—

> "Immemoresque mei disceditis, inquit, Achivi?
> Obrutaque est mecum virtutis gratia nostræ?
> Ne facite, utque meum non sit sine honore sepulchrum,
> Placet Achilleos mactata Polyxena manes."
>
>              Ovid. *Metamorph.*, lib. xiii, Fab. iv.

That the Carthagenians were in the habit of offering up children in sacrifice, a system deduced from their ancestors of Tyre, is but too true. When Gelon, king of Syracuse, conquered the Carthagenian general, Amilcar, he stipulated on granting peace that they should never again sacrifice children to Saturn. The Romans in their treaty with the

---

* Lib. xvii.

same people had a similar stipulation, for which, says Montesquieu, they deserved well of human nature. When the Sicilian tyrant, Agathocles, prepared to besiege the Carthagenians, as they had offered up to their god, Saturn, only the offspring of slaves and strangers, now, in order to avert the impending calamity and to propitiate the god, they sacrificed two hundred of the children of the most illustrious families.* They were placed in the arms of a statue of brass, with a glowing furnace at its feet, into which, on the statue being turned, or the arms sloping downwards, the children fell. Three hundred of the people offered themselves up as a sacrifice at the same time.† They had a law, indeed, by which four children of noble birth were, at stated times, sacrificed to Saturn.‡

The Phœnicians, also, sacrificed infants to their deities.

On experiencing a reverse in Sicily, Hamilcar offered a boy to Kronus ;§ and after Hannibal had gained the battles of Ticinus and Trebia, the senate of Carthage proposed to sacrifice his infant son. In sacrificing to Kronus the mothers embraced their

---

* Diodorus Siculus.
† *True and False Religion*, by Dr. Arnold.
‡ *Anc. Univ. Hist.*, vol. xvii, p. 257.
§ The *Kronus* of the Greeks was the *Moloch* of the Phœnicians.

children, and by kisses and every other means encouraged them, that they might not be appalled at the fearful spectacle. So the Canaanites in sacrificing their children to Moloch drowned their cries by noises. I shall not go into the subject of human sacrifices further than as regards the subjects of this work, infants and children, unless casually. Such sacrifices were practised extensively by people of former ages. The Cyprians, Rhodians, Phoceans, and Ionians, the people of Chios, Lesbos, and Tenedos, had each human sacrifices. So the natives of the Tauric Chersonesus offered up to Diana every stranger whom chance threw on their shore. Hence arose the expostulation of Euripides upon the inconsistency of the proceeding.

The practice of human sacrifice prevailed amongst the nations of the north, the Massagetæ, Scythians, Getes, the Sarmatians, the nations on the shores of the Baltic, especially. The Suevians and Scandinavians offered human sacrifices to their gods Thor and Woden. They worshipped in many places in the isle of Rugen, near the mouth of the Oder, Zeeland, etc., but particularly at Upsal, where they met yearly. They did not spare their own children. Harold, the son of Gunild, the first of that name, slew two of his children in order to obtain a storm of wind to disperse the shipping of Harald, king of Denmark.* Hacon, king of Norway, offered his son in sacrifice to obtain of Odin the victory over the Jomsburg pirates. The most solemn sacrifices were offered every ninth month, and many did not hesitate to offer up their children. Aun, king of Sweden, in order that his life might be prolonged, devoted to the same god the blood of his nine sons. Odin's grove was full of the bodies of men and animals that had been sacrificed.† The ancient kings of Tyre offered their sons in sacrifice in times of danger. To one of them divine honours were paid on that account.

These fearful rites made Plutarch debate within himself whether it might not have been better for the Galatæ and Scythians to have had no conception of any superior beings than to have had notions of gods so thirsting for human blood.‡

These were the customs which the Israelites learned of the people of Canaan, and for which they were upbraided by the psalmist.§

In Rome, paternal authority was sanctioned by Romulus, in its highest degree. The father, violating all natural rights, had absolute power over his children, and could condemn them to

---

* Verstegan, *Antiquities.*
† Mallet's *Northern Antiquities.*
‡ Bryant's *Analysis of Ancient Mythology.*
§ Psalm cv.

death. Exposure and slaughter of children were rife amongst them, these being destroyed and abandoned in various ways ; sometimes being exposed to wild beasts, sometimes thrown into rivers. So it was the custom on a child being born, to place him at the feet of his father, who, on taking him up,* gave a sign that he recognized him ; but, who, on turning his back, proclaimed the doom of the child—death or exposure ; † hence, " tollere filios," to educate : " non tollere," to expose.

The " Twelve Tables " ordained that deformed children should be put to death. The absolute "*patria potestas* " was scarcely modified during the republic, but became restricted under the emperors ; and in later times a parent had not the power of life and death, or of exposing his child. He could sell the child only at the time of birth, or when pressed by extreme want.‡

Diodorus says,§ that in " Toprobana," (believed to be Ceylon), all deformed children were put to

---

* " Terra levasset."

† Adams's *Roman Antiquities*, p. 41. *Dictionnaire Théologique*, par L'Abbé Bergier, Art. *Enfant.*

‡ *A Manual of Civil Law ;* or, *Examination into the Institutes of Justinian.* By P. Cumin, M.A., p. 22.

§ Diod. Sic., lib. 1, cap. 80.

death : so in the kingdom of Sophitus, according to Quintus Curtius.*

With the consent of a father only, could a son acquire property, under the Roman laws ; and his condition was often worse than that of a slave ; as the latter, if sold once became free, which was not the case with the former unless sold three times.†

The power of a father was suspended when a son was appointed to any public office, as in the case of the consul, Spurius Cassius, who, on the expiration of his office, was, it was said, scourged and put to death by his father.‡

Numa is said first to have placed a limit to this power. Augustus interfered as a judge ; and Hadrian transported to an island a jealous parent who assassinated his son, having seized the opportunity of hunting for that purpose.

This power was so unlimited, that neither the age nor the dignity of the offspring could in any way restrict it.§ In the Catiline conspiracy there were several, not at first concerned in it, who went over to Catiline; and amongst these was A. Fulvius, the son of a senator, whom, having been brought

---

* Lib. ix, cap. xi.
† " Si pater filium ter venum dedit, filius a patre liber esto."
‡ Tit. Liv. lib. 2, cap. xli.
§ *Univ. Hist.*, vol. 1, p. 167.

back when on his journey, his father ordered to be put to death.*  This dominion was perpetual, and seems "peculiar to the Roman Jurisprudence." "Jus potestas quod in liberos habemus proprium est civium Romanorum.  Nulli enim alii sunt homines, qui talem in liberos habeant potestatem qualem nos habemus."†

That licentiousness, in progress of time, was extreme, as well as that the practice of abortion was very frequent, we learn from Juvenal; whose revolting description, even allowing all scope for poetical licence and satire, horrifying as it is, must have had a substratum of truth, or a Roman citizen would never have dared thus to libel the masters of the world, and his own country.

> " Hæ tamen et partus subeunt discrimen, et omnes
> Nutricis tolerant, fortunâ urgente, labores
> Sed jacet aurato vix ulla puerpera lecto;
> Tantum artes hujus, tamen medicamina possunt,
> Quæ steriles facit, atque homines in ventre necandos
> Conducit.  Gaude, infelix, atque ipse bibendum
> Porrige quicquit erit: nam si distendere vellet,
> Et vexare uterum pueris salientibus, esses
> Æthiopis fortasse pater; mox decolor hæres
> Impleret tabulas, nunquam tibi mane videndus."
>                                 Juv. *Sat.* vi, v. 592.

---

* Sallust, *Bellum Catalinar.*, cap. **xxxix.**

† Gibbon, vol. iv, p. 231, and *note*, from Patria Potestas in the *Institutes*, lib. 1, tit. iv.  The Pandects and the Code.

In speaking of ladies palming off supposititious children on their husbands, he also alludes to the exposure of infants at the "dirty lakes," where Fortune stood by smiling on the naked outcasts, and wrapping them in her bosom took them to high families :—

 " Transeo suppositos, et gaudia, votaque sœpe
  Ad spurcos decepta lacus, atque inde petitos
  Pontifice salios  *  *  *
 *  *  Stat fortuna improba noctu
  Arridens *nudis infantibus :* hoc fovet omnes
  Involvitque sinu ; domibus tunc porrigit altis."

         *Sat.* vi, v. 601.

A pillar, the *columna lactaria*, was very generally selected in Rome as a place of exposure. A vegetable market was held there, and so the infant stood a good chance of soon being found.

Strange that the elder Pliny could be the apologist for such an unnatural practice as that of abortion amongst the Romans, saying that some women, so prolific were they, would be overstocked with children were this plan not resorted to :— " Quoniam aliquarum fœcunditas plena liberis tali venia indiget."*

Amongst the depraved customs of this luxurious people the crime of killing children *for gain* was not uncommon. It is alluded to by Juvenal when

---

   * Pliny, lib. xxix, cap. 4.

he admonishes orphans to take care of their lives, and to trust to no table, as the meats are warm with maternal poison.* To guard himself against the suspicion of invention, he cites the case of Pontia, the wife of Vettius Bolanus, who poisoned two of her own children at a supper, and was condemned by Nero for the deed.

"Tune duos unâ, sævissima vipera cœna?
Tune duos? septem, si septem forte fuissent.†

The poet says such cruelties might have been perpetrated before, but not for the sake of money—
"Sed non propter nummos."

Holiday, in his illustrations, says Madan, mentions an old inscription on a stone to the following effect, viz., "Here I, Pontia, the daughter of Titus Pontius, am laid, who, out of wretched covetousness, having poisoned my two sons, made away with myself."

Alexander Severus caused the magistrates to hear a father's complaints, and pronounce judgment, in-

---

* "Vos ego pupilli, moneo, quibus amplior est res,
 Custodite animas, et nulli credite mensæ;
 Livida materno fervent adipata veneno."
                                        Sat. vi, v. 628.

† "'Didst thou, O most savage viper, destroy two at one meal?'
 Didst thou, two?
 'Yes, seven, if haply seven there had been.'"
                                        Madan's Juvenal.

P

stead of allowing the power of life and death in the parent's hands; and in the time of Constantine the Great the pains of parricide were inflicted upon those whom the Pompeian law had excepted from penalty in such cases. The dreadful practice of infanticide was even greater in the time of Constantine than in more ancient times, and was rapidly on the increase; apparently owing to distress, the parents preferring to release by death their children from misery than to leave them to the chance of such hardships as they themselves endured. Constantine commanded that all parents in Italy and Africa who could not support their children should get sufficient relief.

On Constantine becoming a Christian he caused to be enacted two laws, both for Italy and Africa, in the years 315 and 322, which exist as yet in the Theodosian Code:* one ordains to furnish funds out of the public treasury to the parent overburthened by children, to take away the temptation of suffocating them, or exposing them to be sold; the second accorded all the rights of property in the exposed infant to those who had the charity to nurse them—a sad memento of the barbarity which existed amongst the Pagans. It is said by Gothfredus that the emperor adopted these

* Codex Theodos., lib. xi, tit. 27.

measures by the advice of Lactantius. The Christian religion reestablished the rights of humanity.* In his reign an attempt was made to stop these murders by visiting the perpetrators with punishment. The first Christian emperors did not venture to punish them strictly as crimes.

The Pompeian and Cornelian laws *de Sicariis et Parricidis* are abridged in the last Supplements of Alexander Severus, Constantine, and Valentinian, in the pandects (or digest) (l. xlviii, tit. viii-ix) and Code (l. ix, tit. xvi-xviii). See likewise the Theodosian Code (l. ix), with Godefoy's Commentary.†

Paulus accounted it murder in the father who strangled, starved, abandoned or exposed his newborn infant.‡

In the third century Tiberius tried to put a stop to the practice, by hanging the priests who presided at those sacrifices on crosses made of trees which shaded their temples.

It was not until the last half of the fourth century, that these infanticides and exposures were put down by the Emperors Valentinian I. (from

---

* *Dictionnaire Théologique*, Bergier, tom. iii, p. 166, art. *Enfant.*

† Bowdler's Gibbon, vol. iv, p. 234, *note.*

‡ Ibidem.

whose cruel disposition so good a movement could scarce be expected), Valens,* and Gratian.

It was much to the credit of the Ancients that in many countries government undertook the care of exposed children. At an early period orphan houses existed both at Athens and at Rome. It would appear as if such places existed in Greece at an earlier period than in Rome. The name so often used by Justinian in his laws regarding charitable institutions, *brephotrophium*,† has a Greek derivation. This emperor, by a special law, in the year 529, declared foundlings to be free. We find little or nothing to guide us as to the manner in which these *brephotrophia* were conducted—either as to nursing, food, clothing, or mortality.

In the 6th century a regular establishment for Orphans existed in Germany, at Triers.‡ In the 7th century there was one at Anjou in France, and St. Magnebodus, bishop of that place, is praised for causing several houses for the rearing of children to be erected. As before mentioned, there was one at Milan, about the year 787. This

---

* See the Code of Justinian, lib. viii, tit. lii, leg. 2. "Unusquisque sobolem suam nutriat. Quod si exponendam putaverit animadversioni quæ constituta est subjacebit."

† Βρεφος, a child; Τρεφω, to educate.

‡ Beckman's *History of Inventions*, vol. ii.

was established by Datheus, at his own expense, in order to stop the crime of child-murder, of which he gives a very affecting account in his letter of foundation. The children were suckled by hired nurses, and educated for seven years. They were also taught trades. In 1168, St. Galdanus took great care of the children exposed in the city of Milan. In 1070, an hospital was founded at Montpellier, by O. de la Trau, and the members, *hospitalarii* sive *spiritus*, entered into an engagement to take care of, and educate foundlings and orphans. They spread quickly in different countries. At Einbeck, an establishment existed in 1272. At Nuremberg, there was one founded in 1331, by a private citizen. The magnificent hospital, the Spedale degl' Innocenti, at Florence, was founded in 1316, by Pollini. The children were suckled by nurses and afterwards received in the house and educated. The girls received portions at their marriage.

The Hospital du S. Esprit, at Paris, was founded in 1362. In 1638, a widow before alluded to, devoted her house to this purpose—called in consequence *Maison de la Couche*. Great abuses took place here—the nurses distorting and maiming the children, in order that beggars might drive a trade by hawking them. St. Vincent de Paul founded in 1640 a new institution, which in 1670 was transferred to the street Notre Dame. This is now the Hôpital des Enfans Trouvés.

But the exposition of children was the prevailing and stubborn vice of antiquity; it was sometimes proscribed, often permitted, almost always practised with impunity by nations which never entertained the Roman ideas of parental power; and the dramatic poets, who appeal to the human heart, represent with indifference a popular custom which was palliated by the motives of economy and compassion. If the father could subdue his own feelings he might escape, though not the censure, at least the chastisement of the laws; and the Roman empire was stained with the blood of infants, till such murders were included by Valentinian and his colleagues in the letter and spirit of the Cornelian law. The lessons of jurisprudence and Christianity had been insufficient to eradicate this inhuman practice, till their gentle influence was fortified by the terrors of a capital punishment."*

The object in exposing children was, first, to avoid the cruelty of murdering them, and next, with the expectation that they should be found

* *History of the Decline and Fall of the Roman Empire. By E. Gibbon, vol. iv, p. 235.*

before death could ensue, and taken to be reared by some charitable person ; and so come by a happier lot than that of their parents. Lactantius gives this as a cause. To this effect certain places of public resort were chosen. Market-places, temples, the meeting of highways, wells, the banks of rivers, or the sea-shore where bathers were likely to congregate, were places well adapted to this end. Even when placed in the water, means were taken, as in China, with a gourd, to secure their floating. Baskets, waterproof bandages, close baskets or small chests were often used.* The penalty for exposing children was at one time death,—a most impolitic law, for people then found it safer to murder them.

In Rome and other places costly ornaments were often appended to the exposed infant, in order to induce people to take them; and in many hospitals and places at the present day tokens of one kind or other are left with the children, sometimes with the hope, in after times, of being able to identify and reclaim them. This was the case at our own Foundling Hospital, and is so in Florence, at the Spedale degl' Innocenti. In this latter place a piece of lead, with a number on it, is appended to the neck of each child, and is long serviceable for identification.

---

* Beckman's *History of Inventions*, vol. ii, p. 437.

Such was the testimony of Gibbon as to the influence of the Christian religion in putting a stop to this nefarious practice, or at all events, even in its infancy, in arresting those horrors which were so widespread and general.

During the fearful persecutions to which the early Christians were subjected, calumnies of all kinds were unsparingly heaped upon them, and amongst the rest it was asserted that they devoured children at their meetings. To this groundless and malignant accusation there were not wanted men who, despite the consequences, hurled back the calumny on the heads of the accusers. Amongst the rest, one of the fathers of the church, Tertullian, in his Apology, eloquently vindicates the Christian cause, and fearlessly tells the persecutors of his faith that it is they themselves who commit the dreadful deeds, secretly and openly, of child-murder, which they try to fasten on the Christians: infants being publicly sacrificed to Saturn in Africa under one of the proconsuls of Tiberius, and the crime being continued in secret up to his own day. "As Saturn," says Tertullian, "did not spare his own children, so does he not spare those of others who by their own parents are offered up, fondling them lest they should be found weeping." It here appears, also, that the modes of death were various—forcing out the breath in water or exposing them to cold and hunger and dogs; dying by the sword, as men would wish to die, being too sweet a death for them. He also shows that amongst Christians it was not lawful to destroy even what was conceived in the womb, and this although the sex could not be ascertained (conception being so recent); as every fruit already existed in the seed.[*]

"How," he exclaims, "can the Christians be charged with homicide, who would be horror-struck not only to take away the life of an infant, but even to prevent its being born, or to expose its life to danger. It is with you this disorder is common. You commit it without fear or remorse." He adds, *that murder is murder in any shape.* This is very different morality to that preached at the Liverpool great meeting of the Social Science Association, and much sounder doctrine to follow.

---

[*] "Quot vultus ex his circumstantibus et in Christianorum sanguinem hiantibus, ex ipsis etiam vobis justissimus et severissimus in nos præsidibus apud conscientias pulsem, qui natos sibi enecent? Siquidem et de genere necis differt; utique crudelius in aqua spiritum extorquatis, aut frigori et fami et canibus exponetis; ferro enim mori ætas quoque major optaverit. Nobis vero, homicidio semel interdicto, etiam conceptum utero dum adhuc sanguis in hominem delibatur, dissolvere non licet. Homicidii festinatio est prohibere nasci; nec refert natam quis eripiat animam, an nascentem disturbet: *homo est, qui est futurus; etiam fructus omnis qui jam in semine est.*"— Tertull. *Apologet.*, lib. ix.

Philo Judeus alludes to this subject and says:—
"If indeed, it seemed reasonable to be at all
influenced by the age, then I think that a person
might very reasonably be even more indignant at
those who slay infants. For when full-grown
people are killed, there may be ten thousand plau-
sible excuses for assaults upon or quarrels with
them, but in the case of mere infants, only just
launched into human life and shown to the light of
day, it is impossible for the greatest liar to invent
an accusation against them ; on which account
those ought to be looked upon as the most inhuman and pitiless of all men, who entertain plots
for the destruction of those infants, and justly
does the sacred law detest such criminals and
pronounce them worthy of death."[*]

He is aided by our other "Apologists," who,
with equal indignation, deny the imputation and
place on the proper shoulders of the Pagans themselves these wicked deeds. S. Justin[†] gives his
assistance and Lactantius[‡] follows on the same
subject. He describes exposure of children as
still prevailing, about the year 331, as a remnant
of barbarity. We find also Minucius Felix, a

---

[*] Philo Judæus, vol. iii (Bohn), p. 333.
[†] Lib. *Apologet.*, i, *n*. 27.
[‡] *Divin. Institut.*, lib. v, cap. 9.

lawyer of the time, boldly and eloquently de-nouncing the crime, and telling the Romans that they exposed their children at one time to wild beasts and birds, and at another time strangled them after, a miserable mode of death. That there are some of them who destroy the origin of the future man in their wombs by medicines, and *commit murder* before they bring forth.*

With the old Germans, in the time of Tacitus,† to set limits to the population by rearing up only a certain number of children and destroying the rest, was considered a flagitious crime. Their man-ners were very virtuous, and the married life was one of much purity, and thus their love for their offspring was very great.‡

Their descendants imposed fines for cruelty to infants; for killing a woman with child, or one not past child-bearing; and passed many decrees for the protection of children. With regard to human sacrifices, although Tacitus says they sacri-ficed human beings to their chief god, Mercury, it

---

* "Vos enim video procreatos filios nunc feris et avibus ex-ponere, nunc adstrangulatos misero mortis genere elidere. Sunt quæ in ipsis visceribus medicaminibus epotis originem futuri hominis extinguant, et parricidium faciant antequam pariant."—*Octav. Minucii Felicis*, cap. xxx, p. 98, Oxon., 1627.

† Tacitus, *Manners of the Germans*, c. xix (Murphy's Tacitus, and *note*).

‡ Salic Law (tit. xxviii, "De Homicidiis Parvulorum").

would appear as if there must be some error in this, as amongst a people so virtuous, and so fond of their wives and children, and with such a desire to have many relatives in old age, human sacrifice was not likely to be offered; and moreover we have the evidence of Cæsar that they had neither Druids to preside over religious rites, nor did they apply their minds to sacrifices.*   At the same time that in speaking of the *Gauls* immediately before (cap. xvi), he says, that in times of troublous visitations, and impending dangers of war, they did not hesitate to sacrifice men, or vow to make such sacrifices, the Druids officiating.   "Aut pro victimis homines immolant, aut se immolaturos vovent, administrisque ad ea sacrificia Druidibus utuntur."   Cæsar, in being thus particular in this distinction between these two people, and having the advantage of personal observation and information, was much less likely to be mistaken in this matter.   Tacitus, however, mentions, that in contradistinction to the Roman custom, the Germans considered child-murder a crime.   Dionysius of Halicarnassus praises the Aborigines for the same reason.†·

---

* "Nam neque Druides habent qui rebus divinis præsint, *neque sacrificiis student.*"—*De Bello Gallico,* lib. vi, c. xxi.

† Lib. i, cap. xvi.

In the fabulous history of the Amazons we are told that men were excluded from their state,—that they held communication with strangers only for the purpose of procreation; murdering their male and preserving their female infants, whose left breasts were cut off to fit them the better for the purposes of war. Few legends of antiquity were so generally believed as that of the Amazons. Most of the old authors believed in the truth of their existence; Homer, Apollonius, Pindar, Herodotus, Isocrates, Plato, and many others notice them, as does Strabo, who expresses a doubt of their existence. They were said to inhabit the shores of the Euxine.

The murder of children was common among the Visigoths, and one of their kings, Chindaswinthus, denounced severe penalties against the perpetrators of the crimes of abortion and murder of children, which were prevalent.*

In the present age Asia seems to be the great hot-bed of infanticide, this being perpetrated in many parts of it—or at all events was so until lately—with the most calculating and cold-blooded indifference. The practice has been known to exist for thousands of years, and has been alluded to by the old historians of Greece and Rome.

---

* *On the History of the Effects of Religion on Mankind.* By the Rev. Edward Ryan.

Hindustan appears to have been some time since the great field of slaughter of female infants. In the account given by Governor Duncan of the measures adopted at Benares for its suppression, we find that it was of frequent occurrence among the tribe of Raj-Kumar, the mothers being obliged to refuse nourishment to the infants. Some of the more wealthy occasionally brought up a daughter; if they had no male children, especially. The shame consequent upon not being able properly to portion them off appears to have been one great cause of their destruction. Mr. Duncan was very successful in suppressing this crime, and had the following engagement drawn up and entered into by the Raj-Kumars :—" Whereas, it hath become known to the government of the Honourable English East India Company, that we of the tribe of Raj-Kumar do not suffer our female children to live ; and whereas this is a great crime, as mentioned in the *Bremah Bywant Purana*,* where it is said that killing even a fœtus is as criminal as killing a Brahmin ; and that for killing a female or woman, the punishment is to suffer in the naraka, or hell, called kat shutala, for as many years as there are hairs on that female's body; and that afterwards that person shall be born

* A sacred mythological poem.

again, and successively become a leper, and afflicted with the jakhima; and whereas the British Government in India, whose subjects we are, hold in detestation such murderous practices, and we do ourselves acknowledge, that although customary among us, they are highly sinful; we do therefore agree not to commit any longer such detestable acts; and among us who shall (which God forbid) be hereafter guilty thereof, or who shall not bring up and get our daughters married to the best of our abilities among those of our own caste, shall be expelled from our tribe, and shall neither eat nor keep society with us, besides suffering hereafter the punishment announced in the above *Purana* and *Sastrœ*.* Dated, December 1789."

In Benares, the tribe of Raj-Kumar deduce their descent from Raja Pit-'hama, in whom ended about 600 years ago, the Chauhan dynasty of the princes of Delhi, and number about 40,000. The custom of female infanticide has been long and is still very prevalent amongst them. The crime is against their religious laws, and they acknowledge its atrocity. It extends also to the Raghuvansa tribe. The difficulty of procuring matches for their daughters is one of the reasons given. A daughter is occasionally spared, but it is generally

---

* A religious ordinance.

in the case of those who have no sons. There are various modes by which, it is said, they put them to death, such as dropping them into a hole filled with milk, &c. This tribe finds wives among other tribes of Rajputs who do not murder their infants. The custom of drowning female infants exists in Kutch, as well as among the Rajput tribes; in the peninsula of Guzerat in the family of Jam of Nagar; in that of Miazeh, or Kalowries of Scinde, and in others. The custom does not extend to illegitimate children, as they will not have to portion such as these. This as to the family of the Rajah, who considers it beneath him to match his daughter with any one; and although the Jarejahs, or collateral descendants of the Rajah, are not obliged to follow the custom, still they generally do through choice. Even the women are not averse to the destruction of their children, but when Musselman prejudices occasionally preserve them, these are afterwards held in the highest contempt, and called *majen*, as intimating that their fathers have degenerated and become pedlars. So savage are some of these women, that even when married to Mahomedans, they continue to practise this, against the religion and wishes of their husbands, in order to advantage the tribe to which they belong. Yet the custom is expressly forbidden by the Hindu law, and is called a great crime in the *Brehma Vyvanta Purana*, where the killing of a fœtus is accounted as great a crime as the killing a Brahmin, and awarding as a punishment an abode in the hell called *Nerka*, during as many years as there are hairs on the body of the child.[*]

It is probable, says Colonel Walker, in his report of the measures adopted by him to put down this nefarious practice, that the custom of Infanticide amongst the Jarejahs was a consequence resulting from the Mahomedan conquest of Scinde, when the greatest part of the inhabitants were obliged to embrace that faith, and thus that the Jarejahs were deprived of the usual mode of disposing of their daughters in marriage, the many other tribes having embraced the new religion. They resisted their invaders until they emigrated into Kutch, where they retained their own religion. They found it difficult to send into countries where their daughters might be affianced to Rajputs of a proper descent, and so consulted their pride, convenience, and superstition, and afterwards the custom became a law, even when they found themselves in a condition to get husbands for their daughters among kindred tribes; and they refused

---

[*] Moore's *Hindu Infanticide*, p. 1-35.

Q

to give up what they considered as a right. Avarice would appear to be one great incentive to the crime, and they do not wish to be at the trouble and expense of settling their daughters in life, which is considerable, if they marry them to their equals; and their pride takes fire at the thought of marrying them to their inferiors. They consider the daughter of a Jarejah should take wealth into the house of her husband, and in those instances where they allow daughters to live, they are influenced by their notions of superiority in giving large portions with their daughters.

The other Rajpoots countenanced infanticide by allowing their daughters in marriage without making any provision for having the females reared. The common mode of death is by putting opium on the nipple, which the child sucks in with the milk, and dies. They also, as another custom, "place the navel string (placenta?) on its mouth, and it expires." The mode by opium and the breast milk may have given rise to the report that the Jarejahs drown their daughters by throwing them as soon as they are born, into a vessel of milk. This seems a popular story, but they are quite careless as to the mode, so that the deed be done. The mother is commonly the executioner of her own children.

The birth of a son is celebrated as a great event amongst the Hindoos of all sorts, while that of a daughter is considered an unfortunate event. The infant is put to death directly it is born, and to kill it, having lived a day or two, would be considered barbarous. Amongst the inhabitants of Scinde, the descendants of Jarejahs who have become Mahommedans, the crime seems to have been discontinued.

The Mahommedan doctrines, says Governor Duncan, "utterly discountenance and severely prohibit so abominable a practice." In Kutch and Kuttawar it was said that the number of female infants yearly murdered amounted to 20,000. This has every appearance of exaggeration, but it is believed that in the peninsula of Guzerat 5,000 perish annually. In Kutch-Hallar and Matsyn Kantha, where there are 150,000 men (the women and children are not counted), the infanticides may be placed at 30,000. Another account gives the number in the above places at 3,100; and Colonel Walker says this number is as short of that destroyed as the former is beyond it.

The Jaitwa Rajputs, following the customs of their conquerors as to infanticide, yet do not deny its sinfulness, and avoid an avowal of the practice. The Hindu religion yet appears very careful to protect women and infants from injury.

With the Raj-Kumars and other tribes of Bengal the practice was prevalent, but has been abolished amongst the Rhatore Rajputs of Jeypore, and Jondpore also, a thing not credited when first reported in Europe. The Jauts and Mewats, tribes of Hindustan, who are a sect of Mussulmans, observe the practice.

Other accounts are also given, says the Rev. Mr. Cormack,* as that, on their Mahommedan invaders seeking their daughters in marriage, their feelings of pride, as well as their policy of throwing off their masters as soon as possible, became alarmed; and as they thought marriages might be insisted on by their invaders, they replied that they did not rear their daughters. The Jarejahs were at this time separated from the other tribes whom they considered worthy of an alliance with them. Their Raj-gurs then proposed death to the children, and offered to become themselves responsible for the guilt. The inhabitants, while they acknowledged the infanticide to be a sin, thought they could transfer the guilt to others, and therefore put it to the account of the Brahminical order. The Raj-gur is literally the priest, tutor, or preceptor of a Rajah, but the name is applied to the domestic Brahmin of any family in Kattywor. The Jahre-

* On Female Infanticide, p. 68, et seq.

jahs formerly obtained wives from the daughters of the numerous races of Rajputs, viz., the Jhalla, Wagela, Wala, and Wadal tribes. For some time they cannot have obtained them, as it is more than a century since any daughters have been seen with them, which speaks sufficiently for female infanticide among them. The means taken by Colonel Walker for putting down this custom has so far succeeded, that what the Jahrejahs looked on formerly with pride, and as a distinction, is now considered infamous and disgraceful; and it is pleasing to know that "natural affection and parental feelings had so far begun to take place of prejudice and superstition as to leave no doubt of the abolition of this inhuman practice." However, as in all heathen nations of antiquity, this custom existed, and among modern nations also; we may fully hope the only great cure for it, the spread of Christianity, may soon throw its cheering light over all parts where such things occur.

What had been so nobly begun by Governor Duncan has been as nobly carried to a successful close by the Viceroy of India, Lord Canning. Recent intelligence from Bombay brings the welcome news that the British Indian Association, which was convened at Oude, declared infanticide to be a great and disgraceful crime. A talookdar, guilty of such a crime, will in future lose caste and may be expelled from the society of his equals. This expression of native opinion is of the utmost importance in marking an epoch in the history of this dread and infamous crime. Humanity may well exult at such a result; and the philanthropist, whose feelings were so often seared by the recital of such deeds of blood in India, such sinful massacres, may breathe in peace, with the fervent hope that the consummation is near at hand, and that India will before long be wholly free from this crime.

Ruling during the terrors of an unexampled mutiny, the wisdom and unerring judgment of Lord Canning brought matters to a triumphant, and it may be hoped a lasting conclusion; and that the last act of his reign should consist in the full vindication of humanity, in putting the finishing stroke to a cruel and barbarous practice, must be to him a matter of great consolation, as it is to his countrymen one of joy and gratitude. Human nature itself, so long outraged, will in the end be fully vindicated; and mothers yet unborn, when they press their girls to their breasts, will bless those who were the cause of their enjoying a mother's greatest happiness. That the two crowning works of Lord Canning's life should be followed by a domestic affliction of a most harrowing nature, in the death of an exemplary wife, the sharer of his anxieties and troubles, his joys and hopes, is one of those dispensations of providence for which the Christian must be prepared; and an event in which his countrymen can only offer their deep and unaffected sympathy.

Neither must Sir John Lawrence be forgotten amongst those benefactors of their race who grappled with this evil in India. What Lord Canning did for Oude, Sir John had already done for Lahore, when the tribes who practised infanticide were called together and induced to acknowledge that the custom of which they long had been guilty was a great sin, and might be put a stop to. The portions to be given in marriage, and which were not to be exceeded, were agreed upon, and a girl could not in future lose caste by marrying an inferior. This losing of caste, among the Rajputs, as before mentioned, was the great cause of female infanticide; so great was the portion expected with a girl, and so great was the shame if through poverty she should marry a person below her own grade.

One of the darkest traits in the national character of the Chinese, is the prevalence of at least *female* infanticide. With regard to the extent to which this is systematically practised, authorities are at variance.* In the hopes of a plentiful harvest, children are yearly cut in two or poisoned; or are often thrown into the river as sacrifices to the water. That the practice of child-selling and infanticide takes place to a very great extent is certain. Slavery is supplied by the great sale of children by their parents. Parents also sell their children for the purposes of prostitution. At Kin-Sai those prostitutes were in such numbers that Marco Polo dared not make the true report, but says that in another city there were twenty-five thousand.†

A large proportion of female children are drowned—the custom is general, and the horrid deed is performed with the greatest levity. No compunctious feelings seem to actuate the murderer. To ask one of their magnates whether he has female children, is considered offensive and rude. The father has authority, and exercises it as he thinks proper, over the lives of his children.‡

Gutzlaff says that the infanticide of female children is not uncommon. This takes place at

* Conder's *Modern Traveller :* see Morrison's *View*, pp. 124-5.

† *Univ. Hist.*, vol. i.

‡ *Journal of Three Voyages to the Coast of China.* By Gutzlaff, p. 149.

the time of, or shortly after birth. The fathers
are the murderers, and they need only pretend that
the sufferings during life's struggles of their children
are thus prevented.*

As if to guard against a return on the part of
children of this cruelty, filial duty is strongly
enjoined by the Chinese laws, as it was amongst
the Romans, who enjoyed such absolute power
over their children ; and the great Chinese philo-
sopher, Confucius, in laying down, as necessary, an
entire submission to the divine will ; and as an
earnest of this, demanding unlimited obedience to
the law of the state, could scarcely have anticipated any general countenance to a practice which
sets all law, divine and human, at defiance. Indeed, the extreme veneration, amounting to idolatry,
of the Chinese for their parents, might well plead
to the hard hearts of parents to spare their
offspring. This strong feeling was carried so far,
unhappily, that it was accompanied with human
sacrifices until about a century ago.† Punishment
of children may be carried even to a fatal termina-
tion, and sexual mutilation of males is practised as
a means of getting promotion in the offices of the
state. *And all this while the penal law prohibits*

* *Sketch of Chinese History.* By C. Gutzlaff.
† *Univ. Hist.,* Art. *Confucius.*

*infanticide!* In Pekin and Canton Sir George Staunton found the exposure of children a very frequent occurrence, owing to extreme poverty. Yet religion favours the rearing of children in China.*

Du Halde also says, that the custom of exposing children in the streets of Pekin and Canton is very common. They consider inattention to life criminal only when the child is endowed by time with mind and sentiment. A faint hope seems to be entertained that life may be preserved by those appointed to collect these unfortunate female children; for it is females who are generally exposed, as the males will be more likely afterwards to contribute to the support of their unnatural parents. From one of the pious missionaries, not likely to exaggerate, it was learned that in Pekin about two thousand were yearly exposed—a large portion perishing.†

Facfur, a prince of the province of Mangi, is said to have saved children exposed through the poverty of their parents, to the amount of twenty thousand annually. He had the boys brought up to some trades, and married to females similarly

---

* Macartney's *Embassy to China*, vol. ii.
† *Embassy to China*, vol. ii, p. 158.

reared. "Rex tamen infantes, quos sic colligi jubet, tradit divitibus quibusque, quos in regno suo habet ; præsertim illis qui liberis carent, et ut in adoptionis suscipiant filios mandat. Eos verò quos ipse nutrit, matrimonio tradit puellis ejusdem conditionis." In the reign of Kang-Hi, Pekin had an establishment for infants so exposed. (About 1720.*)

"In the penal code of the Chinese, murdering father, mother, son, uncle, etc., is duly denounced, p. 322, but a daughter seems to have been overlooked";† or, rather, intentionally left out.

The duties of filial piety, however, are so strictly enjoined, that a man a few years since was put to death for having beaten his mother, as was also his wife for having assisted him. The house in which the crime was perpetrated was considered unfit to be the habitation of any human being, and was destroyed from the foundation.‡

The crime amongst the Chinese, however, forms some contrast to it as it existed amongst the Romans. With the former, poverty is the ruling incentive ; with the latter, lust of power only.

---

* *Travels of Marco Polo.* By T. Wright, Esq., M.A., p. 295, and *note.*

† Moore's *Hindu Infanticide*, p. 272.

‡ Corner's *China*, p. 193.

This view, Sir George Staunton, in his work, *Ta Tsing Leu Li*, seems to take.

Malthus thinks the crime is only perpetrated in China owing to great poverty, and says, during a residence of several months in Canton, he never saw a case; and yet he says many thousands of the poorest classes live entirely on the water. In casting a child into the water they sometimes fasten a gourd to it, by which it floats. It is sometimes saved by this means by the compassionate. Malthus considers this a sign of care rather than of criminality; as he saw a child thus floating! Save us from our friends!

There is a foundling hospital at Macao endowed by the Portuguese, and many poor outcast children are there cared for.

Barrow has computed, upon the best authority, that of the female children of the Chinese 9000 are exposed in Pekin, and as many in the provinces. He states that the number of children thus inhumanly exposed, slaughtered, or interred alive, is stated by different authors to be from 10 to 20,000 annually, throughout the empire.[*] Medhurst considers the prevalence of infanticide connected with economical rather than religious considerations; females being so generally the victims

---

[*] Barrow, *Travels in China*, p. 167; Bohn's *Marco Polo*.

as being more costly in the rearing, and inasmuch as they are less likely to succeed in the battle of life, and so make the desired return.*

It is thought, says the Abbé Bergier, that amongst the Chinese every year 30,000 are put to death at their birth. The parents expose them in the highways, where they are trampled to death by animals, or devoured by vultures. Others are put to death under the influence of superstition, or are smothered for the purpose of avoiding the trouble of rearing them.

In the island of Formosa, says Mandelslo, the women believe it would be a sin and a shame to have children until they are 35 or 36 years old. Their priestesses inculcate this belief, and assist those pregnant in procuring abortion by violent means.†

In Tonkin the crime of abortion is very prevalent, and there are women whose profession it is to facilitate and cause it.‡

It is mentioned by many writers that the Mahommedan invaders of different countries did at all events one service, that of prohibiting child-murder. Colonel Walker remarks, as the custom of infanti-

---

* *China, its State and Prospects.* By W. H. Medhurst, p. 43.

† Mandelslo's *Voyages and Travels*, p. 170.

‡ *Edinburgh Encyclopedia*, vol. xii, p. 118.

cide could be so generally traced among nations, that one benefit resulting from the imposture of Mahomet consisted in "the abolition of so inhuman an usage among his followers;" and certainly the Koran expressly forbids the crime. "Kill not your children for fear of being brought to want; we will provide for them and for you: verily, the killing of them is a great sin."* It is believed that from the injunctions and prohibitions of Mahomet the practice of infanticide was put a stop to amongst the ancient Arabians, who were in the habit, especially the Koreish and Kendal tribes, of destroying their daughters from inability to rear them, or from fear that they might bring shame on them by immorality.

Mahomet alludes to the effect produced amongst the Arabs on the birth of a daughter—"and when any of them is told the news of the birth of a female, his face becometh black and he is deeply afflicted; he hideth himself from the people, because of the ill tidings which have been told him, considering within himself whether he shall keep it with disgrace, or bury it in the dust." And it is a curious fact that up to the present day, while the birth of a male child occasions a general shooting and shouting among the Arabs and the inhabitants of

* *The Alcoran of Mahomet,* by Sale, vol. ii, p. 116.

the eastern shores of Africa, a dead silence prevails if *an "insignificant infant"* is born.* The idolatrous Koreish, according to some, bury their daughters upon a mountain, Abu Dalamah, near Mecca.†

Indeed, a similar feeling as regards the birth of female children appears to exist in China, India, Arabia, Persia, and other places.

Yet it would appear, from many authors, that the Mahommedans allow the practice of infanticide, but that its frequency is lessened by the universal system of procuring abortion, a crime so strictly of a pagan character. In the large bazaars of British India are persons who sell and administer drugs for the purpose of destroying children before birth. The midwives who attend the Turkish women are said to be Jewesses, and are considered very expert at procuring abortion without injuring the constitutions of the mothers; and this is done when a woman has once had two or three children.‡ Blacquiere thinks that the bashaw of Tripoli encouraged his wives to procure abortion.

Dr. Bryce remarks, that these Jewish-Turkish women "all pretend to possess, and some have

---

* *True and False Religion*, by J. M. Arnold, D.D., p. 283.
† *Ancient History of the Jews*, p. 837.
‡ Slade's *Travels in Turkey.*

become famous and wealthy by their pretentions, certains means, not only to obviate sterility, but also to procure abortion by administration of drugs—a practice avowedly tolerated, and often resorted to by Turkish women, both from their dislike to frequent pregnancy, and from command of their lords, when their harem threatens to become too numerous.[*]

Sir John Chardin says, that the Mahommedan Tartars, when they cannot maintain their children, think it a charity to murder them when newly born, as well as those sick and past recovery. It is said also by others that child-murder is considered a matter of very little moment in Turkey; and that the offspring of the younger princes of the royal family, who are generally kept in honourable confinement, are destroyed at birth.[†]

The daughters of the pagan Arabs, according to some accounts, were allowed to live until their sixth year, and of any one whom it was resolved to put to death, the father said to the mother, "Perfume her and adorn her, that I may carry her to her mothers'." The father took her to a

---

[*] *Sketch of the State and Practice of Medicine at Constantinople*, by C. Bryce, M.D., *Edinburgh Med. and Surg. Journal*, vol. xxxiv, pp. 8-9.

[†] *The Present State of Turkey*, etc. By T. Thornton.

deep well, and standing behind desired her to look down. He then pushed her headlong into it, and filling up the pit levelled it with the rest of the ground. Other accounts have it that when a woman was on the verge of labour, a pit was dug and she was delivered on its brink; and if a daughter happened to be born she was thrown into the pit.

Sasaa, the grandfather of Al Farasdak, frequently redeemed female children from death. For each child he gave two female camels and a he camel.

The ancient Syrians sacrificed to Jupiter and Juno, crowning their victims with garlands and driving them out of the temple, on one side of which was a deep precipice, where they perished; and some tied up their children in sacks and threw them down the same precipice.* They also sacrificed on the tombs of their kings the dearest of their wives and concubines, as well as persons who had deserved well of the state. The domestics of a departed king, to the number of fifty, together with the same number of horses, were offered up.

The Ionians held an annual feast in honour of Diana Tricolaria, instituted by the Athenians, at which they sacrificed a male and female child;†

---

* *Ancient History of the Jews*, etc., p. 482.
† Ibidem, p. 548.

R

and Pliny informs us, that when the Mysian city, Abydus, was besieged by Philip, King of Macedon, the inhabitants in their frenzy put their wives and children to death, and then killed themselves.

Human sacrifices are not near so common in India since the intervention of Europeans, and especially English, as well as since the Mohammedan influence prevailed; but until very recent times discoveries were made which showed that such had taken place in secret; and indeed, my late friend, Mr. Cole of the East India Company's Service, informed me that up to his period (about eight years ago) the women killed their children when out of the reach of European influence. This also Sir W. Sleeman shows in his late work on Oude. They use a decoction of the Datura Stramonium.

Sir John Bowring and Dr. Williams show that the practice is still very extensive, and that there are towers made of brick or stone where unfortunate children, chiefly female, are thrown by their parents into a hole made in the side of the wall.

In the north of Bengal, if an infant refuses to be suckled, or declines in health, it is placed in a basket, which is hung on a tree. It is usually destroyed by ants or by birds before the period when it can be again taken down. At Gango Sagor the women were accustomed to throw their infants into the

water in fulfilment of some solemn vow; and considered the sacrifice not propitious unless a shark or
other sea monster swallowed it before their eyes.

At the siege of Ispahan, by an Affghan army,
in 1722, during the famine which ensued, the
most loathsome articles of food failing, the inhabitants were driven to the terrible resource of eating
human flesh.* The siege lasted from March to the
end of October. Towards the end of August a
horse's carcase sold for one thousand crowns. Dogs,
though esteemed unclean, were greedily devoured,
as long as they could be obtained. The leaves
and bark of trees, and leather afforded a partial
supply. At last "the citizens slew each other, and
parents murdered their children to furnish the
horrid meal." All who tried to escape were murdered by the Affghans.†

It is said that in Egypt the practice of abortion
and infanticide prevails very much, particularly
the former, and that there are professors for that
purpose amongst the women; and at Cairo, Arabian
physicians follow, and have long followed, this
horrid practice as a profession. Infanticide is
seldom visited with punishment, and a girl who
becomes pregnant, in case she destroys the fœtus,

---

* Conder's *Modern Traveller, Persia*, p. 194.
† Malcolm, vol. i, p. 641.

has only to liberate a male or female slave. A married woman, in case she kills her new-born infant, cannot be punished unless two witnesses have seen her do it; and if convicted, she has to pay a fine to her husband, or he may imprison her. She may free herself by oath, in case there is suspicion only.*

Amongst the Gagas, children are destroyed at their birth, by being buried alive. The people rear no children of their own, but when they take a town, they take the boys and girls, and adopt them as their own. Sierra de Leon was the natural country of these Gagas, whence they came about the year 1540. In undertaking any great enterprise they kill a male child.†

The Niam-Niams, or Ghilanes (their name signifies cannibals), an African race residing probably about the sources of the Nile, are said to immolate victims to the sources of a great river. They immolate their prisoners aud eat them without distinction; but prefer women and children. They often seek quarrels with neighbouring negro tribes, and devour their children without pity. Formerly, the Arabs bought from the Djelabs, or slave dealers,

---

* *Letter on the State of Legal Medicine in Egypt, in Annales d'Hygiène.*

† Pinkerton's *Voyages and Travels*, vol. xvi, p. 326.

great numbers of them, but now do not, as the
children, overcome by the ferocious instincts of
their nature, on growing up devoured the children
of their masters.*

The laborious care of children depending on
mothers, and in the savage state the hardships and
distresses are so great, that women in some parts
of America procure frequent abortions by the use
of certain herbs.† To prevent a numerous offspring, it is universal for the American women to
suckle a child for several years; as it would, in
their wild life be otherwise difficult to rear two
children at a time.‡ For the same reason, when
twins are born one of them is destroyed; and
when a mother dies while nursing a child, it is
buried with her in the same grave; as in New
Holland, when all hopes of rearing it are given
up. Yet all this results from the difficulties of
their position, as parental affection and attachment
are not uncommon amongst them.

In the Kurile islands it is usual to destroy
one of twins, and some of the American Indians
do so under the impression, in such cases, of infi-
delity on the part of the mother. Amongst the

---

* *Voyage au Pays des Niam-Niams.*
† Robertson's *Hist. of America*, vol. i, p. 297.
‡ Ibid., p. 322.

Kamtschadales also, one of twins is destroyed : the mothers even threw their children alive to the dogs. From superstitious feelings children born during a storm are destroyed. Conjurations, however, may avert this.

In Kamtschatka, according to Krascheninikow's "History of Kamtschatka," herbs and conjurations are used in order to prevent conception, and poisonous medicines to procure abortion, in which skilful old women assist. M'Kensie says, the women of Knisteneaux frequently procure abortion, from fear of the distress consequent on having children to rear ; and Ellis says, that the Esquimaux along the shores of Hudson's Bay, oblige their wives to cause frequent abortions by means of an herb common to the country ; while Denys asserts that women of North America, if pregnant while suckling, caused abortion : one child being considered sufficient to support at once.* In some parts of America, the natives, seized with dismay at the ravages of the small pox, kill their children.

Many children are annually destroyed amongst the American savages. The Choctaws sometimes bury the infants alive as soon as they are born ; sometimes they strangle them, sometimes press upon their breasts.

* *Edinburgh Encyclop.*, vol. xiii, p. 19.

Beltrami says, public sacrifices are considered indispensable by the Indians, when deliberating on the question of war or peace. Some of the prisoners are sacrificed to their Manitons of war, or their infernal gods.*

The North-American Indians are spoken of very favourably, by some writers, as regards infanticide. Mr. Herkewelder, who was long in the mission of the United Brethren, says he never knew of any tribe of Indians amongst those in Pennsylvania and the neighbouring states who killed their children, when deformed or distorted. Similar testimony is given by Franklin, who says, when an occasional infanticide takes place, it is looked upon with great abhorrence, and as a great crime. In this he is joined by Dr. Richardson, who says that the Cree Indians consider the crime of infanticide will be punished hereafter; believing that the women who commit it never reach the mountain —by which they mean their heaven; "but are obliged to hover round the seats of their crimes, with branches of trees tied around their legs." Charlevoix,† however, describes some of the North-

---

* *Journey to the Shores of the Polar Sea, with a brief Account of the Second Journey in* 1825-27. By John Franklin, R.N., vol. i, p. 151.

† *Journal d'un Voyage à l'Amérique Septentrionale*, vol. iii, p. 335.

American savages, who destroy all infants that
lose their mothers before they are weaned. They
think no other woman can nurse them properly.

In Greenland, if a mother dies, and leaves a
helpless babe behind her, if the father have no one
to nurse it, he cannot endure to see the infant's
distress. He buries it alive along with its mother.
They are wrapped up in skins, carried to some
high place, and covered with broad stones to keep
off the birds and foxes.

The inhabitants about Hudson's Bay very commonly procure abortion by the use of an herb.*
In Labrador the widows and orphans were often
put to death through fear of being unable to provide support for them.† Miguel Venegas says,
that in California mothers destroy their offspring
owing to a scarcity of food, and that Father Salva
Tierra gave a double allowance to women recently
delivered in order to stop the crime.

In ancient Mexico, where human sacrifice was
very great, almost fabulous numbers are given by
different authors. Torquemada asserted that 20,000
children were sacrificed annually, exclusive of other
victims.‡

---

* Ellis's *Voyage to Hudson's Bay*, p. 198.
† Barrow's *Account of a Journey in Africa.*
‡ *Mon. Ind.*, lib. vii, c. 21.

Zumurraga, the first Bishop of Mexico, and the most respectable authority in favour of such high numbers, in a letter to the Chapter-General of his order, 1631, says that the Mexicans sacrificed 20,000 children, exclusively of other victims, annually. But on an inquiry made, according to B. Diago del Castello, by the Franciscan monks sent into New Spain, it was found that about 2,500 were yearly sacrificed.\* At the end of every month, or twenty or thirty days, they sacrificed some captives. When corn of all kinds began to germinate, they sacrificed on a hill to Flaloch, the god of waters, a boy and a girl about three years old. These bloody sacrifices were renewed when the corn was grown up about two feet high; when they sacrificed to the same god four children of six or seven years old. They used also to drown a boy and a girl in the lake, with much ceremony; sending them, as they said, to keep company with the gods of the lake.†

In opposition to all these, B. de la Casas asserts that the Mexicans never sacrificed more than 50 or 100 in a year.‡

The South American women on the Orinoko are

---

\* Robertson's *History of America*, vol. ii, p. 481.

† Picart's *Religious Rites of all Nations*, p. 751.

‡ *Brevissima Relacion*, p. 105.

kept in such a state of abject misery, says Gunilla, that in order to spare their daughters the same fate they cause them to perish by cutting the navel string too close. Amongst the Raudales, on the banks of that river, the scourge was said to be almost unknown; but amongst the curses of this part is the guilty practice of preventing pregnancy by deleterious herbs. Among the Abiponians, a South American tribe, Dobrizhoffer* knew mothers who destroyed the whole offspring immediately on birth.† The Araucanians, a powerful nation of Chili, allow fathers and husbands to kill their children and wives.‡ In Guiana, amongst some of the half-civilized islands, young wives dread becoming mothers from the dangers to which their offspring become exposed; and when twins are born, it is necessary, from a false sense of family honour, that one should be destroyed.§ Rats, opossums, and such like only, they say, should bring forth a great number of young at a time; and they think that two children born at the same time cannot belong to the same father. If a new born infant have any deformity, or be of a feeble constitution,

---

* *Edinb. Encyclop.*, vol. 12, p. 119.
† *De Abiponibus*, tom. ii, p. 105.
‡ *Edinb. Encycl.*, Art. *America*.
§ Robertson's *History of America*, vol. ii, p. 481.

it is put to death by the father, who will pretend that he lost such children by natural deaths. These murders, however, are said by some to be less frequent than they are believed to be.*

The Peruvians sacrificed children on different occasions, as on the sickness of the Inca ; in disappointments in war and other matters ; ten being in such cases offered up, as we learn from Acosta. In case of the sickness of a father, he offers up his son to Viriachocha (or the sun), in hopes of saving his own life. Two hundred children were offered up on the coronation of an Inca. It is said that they even exceed the Mexicans in the slaughter of children. Robertson, who, in his *History of America*, eulogises the mildness of the manners of the Peruvians, and endeavours to show that Acosta was in error, yet admits that at one of their festivals "they offer cakes of bread moistened with blood drawn from the arms, eyebrows, and noses of their children"; and he considers this rite may have been *derived from the ancient practice of sacrificing human victims.*

The dearest of their own children in some parts of the country, have been offered up by the inhabitants as most acceptable to their deities, and as

* *Personal Travels to the Equinoctial Regions of America.* By Alex. von Humboldt (Bohn's *Scientific Library*, p. 248).

said by Burder (*Oriental Customs*, No. 1146), was the practice of the inhabitants of Florida, the victim being always a male infant.

In Collins's *New South Wales*, some melancholy instances of female misery are given, and strangely enough, for a Christian, he says, "The condition of these women is so wretched that I have often on seeing a female child anticipated the miseries to which it was born, and thought *it would be a mercy to destroy it.*"* If the mother die the father places the helpless infant in the same grave, which, a large stone being thrown into it, is filled up. It was believed that this practice was generally prevalent. The reason usually given was, that none could be found who would rear such child, and that, therefore, it must undergo greater miseries by being allowed to live. This, Malthus says, b. i, c. 3, points to the great difficulty of rearing children in savage life, where the women, being the drudges, cannot bring up two children at the same time. They have recourse, in order to procure abortion, to violent compression of the body of the mother, who frequently dies in consequence of the injury sustained.

In New Holland the mother suffocates the weakest and worst-developed child; and here, too,

* Vol. i, p. 607.

when a mother dies, the infant is invariably placed by the father in the same grave. In case of twins of different sexes it is always the female that is killed.

In New Zealand infanticide is common. The mother frequently kills the child "by placing her fingers on the soft parts between the joinings of the skull."*

Captain Cook† inferred that the Otaheitans occasionally offered human sacrifices ; and having read the account of Bougainville, he witnessed on his third voyage a human sacrifice in Otaheite. In this case the victim was a middle-aged man of the lowest class. Cook believed that such things happened frequently throughout the islands of the Pacific.

The Otaheitans in some cases seem to have the power of life and death over their children ; as, in the case of a couple cohabiting, the man may not only make a new choice, but kill the child. They do not consider it any crime to murder their own children, and their chief does not interfere, as they seem to have a perfect right "to do what they like with their own."*

Cook found the population of Otaheite, in 1776,

---

* Cruise's *Journal*, p. 290.    † Cook's *Voyages*, vol. i, p. 185.
‡ Mavor's *Voyages*, vol. ix, ch. ix.

some 20,000, but in the beginning of this century,
or about thirty years afterwards, it was reduced to
5,000 or 6,000, and this chiefly owing to the practice of murdering the infants. Mr. Ellis* asserts
that every mother he met with imbrued her hands in
the blood of her offspring while idolatry prevailed.
When the Otaheitan chief has a child by a woman
of an inferior order it is always killed; and with
the higher ranks of females all their natural children must perish. It was considered that two-
thirds of the children were destroyed before the
introduction of Christianity.†

Doubtless some other causes than that of infanticide were in operation, thus to thin the
population of Otaheite; such as fevers, dysentery,
pulmonary consumption, &c. Since the introduction of Christianity, this barbarous custom has
been abolished. The simple manners of the inhabitants of some of the South Sea Islands, were
not accompanied with equal innocence or stainless
conduct. Their ferocity in their wars was extreme,
and they were in the habit of eating their enemies.
Their god, Etoo, had human sacrifices offered to
him, and polygamy was generally practised by men
and women. Daughters were prostituted for hire,

---

* *Polynesian Researches*, vol. i, p. 198.
† Turnbull's *Voyages Round the World in* 1800, etc.

and the person hiring might, if he chose, either keep the woman or put her away, and kill the children. The Europeans, says Turnbull,* here caused the unhappy inhabitants to be visited with syphilis, which destroys a great number; but even this is not so effective in depopulating the country as the practice of infanticide and human sacrifices.

Should this go on, it is added, the country must soon become a desert. In two towns of the missionaries the calculation was in the first, seven thousand, but in the last five thousand inhabitants only. Peculiar societies exist, the Eareeoie societies, the characteristics of which seem to be " promiscuous intercourse and infanticide." According to Mr. Anderson, as quoted by Malthus, the most beautiful of both sexes thus spend their lives amongst those dreadful enormities. These societies, according to Captain Cook, consist of the higher classes, numbering the royal family among them, whose increase is thus prevented. The very low ebb at which their morals exist, may be judged from the fact of the king's wife having borne two children by her attendants; and of Edeah, his mother, having had several since her separation from Pomarrie. These were all strangled the moment after birth. Being the offspring of base connection, they do not con-

* Vol. iii, pp. 68, 77, 1800-4.

sider the act criminal. Children on being born, are suffocated, a piece of cloth, dipped in water, being applied to their mouths and noses.

From these societies of the higher classes the custom has spread among the lower. It seems even to be resorted to more *as a fashion than from poverty, and is practised without reserve.* In some degree to vindicate the character of the Otaheitans, Mr. Moore mentions that he heard Sir Joseph Bankes say he never saw more sorrow evinced than by one of these women, when "reciting the sad necessity she was under of destroying her child;" and says that the Raj Kumar females evinced a similar feeling in their gratitude to Mr. Duncan, on relieving them from the pangs attendant on such a custom.

In Easter Island the great disproportion of males to females, would argue a custom of infanticide, although on the visit of Perouse sufficient grounds for proof were not obtained.

In the Marianne Islands there appeared to be a similar society to the Eareeoie of Otaheite; and in the island of Formosa women were not allowed to bring children into the world before the age of 35, abortion being effected by a priestess before that time. The operation is said to be attended with great danger and pain.

In the Sandwich Islands the crime is unhappily common. In some of the islands nearly two-thirds of the children perish by the hands of their parents during the first or second year of their age. Among the Otaheitans the infant was generally spared if it survived a few hours. The grave is often already prepared at the time of birth, and the child being placed in it they throw earth over it, and trample it to a level. The crime is not even owing to distress, for it is often provoked by the necessity of half an hour's additional labour in the day for the child's support ; and even when it interferes with the hours of pleasure of the mother.*

It is said by Dr. Ruschenberger† that the crime is not so prevalent latterly ; nor is it openly committed. Children are now destroyed at the fourth or fifth month of pregnancy, almost entirely in cases of illegitimacy, to the great peril of the mothers. Infanticide has been made a crime by the civil law.

In Paragoa, one of the Philippine Islands, Gemelli Careri says that children, who from imperfect formation may not be able in after life to support themselves, were placed alive in a hollow cane and

---

* *A Residence in the Sandwich Islands*, by C. S. Stewart, p. 192, Boston ed.

† *Voyage Round the World from* 1835 *to* 1838.

S

thus buried. In Japan they suffocate their children when too poor to bring them up.

In Ceylon and Madagascar children are killed should the priests and astrologers declare the epoch of their birth unfortunate; and certain periods and days are judged ominous. The child is left to be devoured by wild beasts, or to perish from cold or by ants.* The first female child is generally preserved, and all the males. It is rare in those districts where the practice prevails to find more than one female child in a family.†

Other places might be mentioned where infanticide was practised, but enough has now been said to show its prevalence and extent in different times; and more than enough it may be hoped to render the crime in any shape or form more and more repulsive.

---

* *Narrative of a Journey through the Upper Provinces of India*, etc. By Bishop Heber.

† *Notes of the Medical Topography of the Interior of Ceylon.* By H. Marshall, Surgeon to the Forces.

# INDEX.

FINIS.

---

ERRATUM.

Page 39, line 19, *for* " healthy," *read* " unhealthy."

www.ingramcontent.com/pod-product-compliance
Lightning Source LLC
Chambersburg PA
CBHW081413270326
41931CB00015B/3258